SOMEONE ELSE'S SHOES

SOMEONE ELSE'S SHOES

Walking the Muddy Path Toward Personal Sovereignty

MARYBOB STRAUB

Printed in the United States of America

First Printing, 2019

ISBN-13: 978-1-943625-89-5
print edition

ISBN-13: 978-1-943625-90-1
ebook edition

DreamSculpt Books and Media
An imprint of
Waterside Productions
2055 Oxford Ave
Cardiff, CA 92007
www.DreamSculpt.com

I dedicate this book to my parents, Rosemary and Bob Hogenkamp, who taught me to love people, to my husband, Bill, who continues to teach me to love me, and to my children, Kelly and Lara Rose, who have taught me that love makes anything possible.

ACKNOWLEDGEMENTS

This book sat inside of me for decades waiting to be ready for words. It was my husband and biggest fan, Billy, who first asked me to write it all down. Emory University's Linda Clopton encouraged and supported me to forge ahead, and I have learned to become a dream builder from my benevolent mentor, Mary Morrissey. My publisher, Lynn Kitchen, wrapped her loving words and arms around me, providing a safe place for me to land in my moments of angst. My editor Jared Rosen, always only a phone call away, walked this path with me. His intuition, guidance, appreciation of my stories and response to my jokes kept this stew cooking. Without him this would all still be inside my head. Editor and guide, Patricia Bukur, revealed to me the depth of my story and shined a light on old thought patterns waiting for release. Special thanks to my dear friends Debe, Julie, Kathy, Melissa, Paul, Miranda, Judi, and Chiquita who encouraged me every step of the way. This book was definitely a group effort, and I will be eternally grateful for every moment with these people.

I want to express that same depth of gratitude to all of the players in my story, those whom I appreciated at the time and those whom I did not. Without the touch of each of them, my ship might have sailed a very different course, and each gust of wind led to here.

CHAPTERS

OF MILK AND HONEY

"Home is where the heart is." – Pliny the Elder

Relish Trays and Caskets in the Living Room

I was certain the family in the Norman Rockwell painting *Freedom from Want* was ours. Over forty years of it being just that, then one decision changed everything. Or was it really only one? The all-American scene portrays a model matriarch in her white apron serving a traditional Thanksgiving turkey to her tight-knit family. In the far-left corner of the table is a young girl with an innocent smile ear to ear. That little one was me. Our Thanksgiving and Christmas dinners were exactly like that, and our living room was the scene of numerous social gatherings. My mom and dad had lots of friends, and my mother loved to prepare relish trays for their guests. Sweet gherkin pickles were her favorites. No kidding. They barely made it from the jars to the beautifully arranged tables.

The scene would eventually change. I think we would all agree that we never saw it coming. My family and friends could have been the models for Mr. Rockwell as he brushed the paint onto that canvas in 1943, only it would have been twenty years later. That would make me nine years old, the baby of the family with two siblings, nine and twelve years older. My mother always referred to me as "a pleasant surprise," having arrived four years after their loss of another baby girl. My mother was weeks away from forty years old at my birth, and my fortunate placement in the sibling lineup was a blessing for me. I'm pretty sure that she and my dad were shocked beyond words at the realization they were pregnant again. The name they blessed me with was the same as that of my still-born sibling, *Mary Roberta*, to be known as *Mary Bob*. Mary came from my mother Rosemary, and Roberta from my father Robert. For many years, it was two words until I decided to connect them to avoid being called *Mary*. Those close to me chuckle when someone now calls me Mary. It's a sure sign that the someone and I are *not* closely connected. I have always loved my name. Add my former husband's last name Straub, and it takes on a cadence all its own.

As *normal* as I believe my childhood to have been, there are some who may tilt their heads slightly when I mention my experience of also having dead bodies in our living room. It didn't happen often, but it wasn't rare either. "Why?" You might ask. My mother was an elementary school teacher, and she and my father owned a funeral home. Occasionally, there were too many "showings" for the number of rooms in the funeral home, so the deceased and the family were welcomed into our living room until one of the other spaces became available. After teaching school all day, my mom came home, made supper, corrected her students' papers, went to the funeral home to "fix the hair" or visit the family of the deceased, came back home, sat at the kitchen table and talked with me, all before she went to bed. So many times, she worried about having said or done something "not quite right" for the families. She would review her recent conversations over and over until she was satisfied that her every move had been situationally appropriate. Her energy was boundless, her mind never stopped, and how she did it all is beyond me.

My dad came from a long line of funeral directors. My great-grandfather arrived from Holland in 1874 and started a furniture/funeral home business in another small town nearby. My dad's schooling was delayed due to his inability to speak English. He always described his language as "low German." The "furniture/undertaker" combo seemed to be a not-so-unusual blending of occupations back in the day. Makes sense, I guess. I mean a casket is a sort of *furniture* I suppose.

The permanent location of my parent's funeral home had been decided upon after having been ousted by their former neighbors in another part of town. In the old neighborhood, petitions had been signed, and my family was ordered by the city court to move their business. Apparently, a funeral home on the block was not viewed as an asset. Forty years later my mother would answer the front door of the house at that "new" location. Only strangers came to the front door, so on that particular day we didn't know who was ringing the bell. Outside the screen stood a man looking mournful. He asked my mother if she were Mrs. Hogenkamp, and when she replied, "yes," the tears began pouring down his cheeks. He said, "I've come to apologize. Many years ago, I signed a petition to have your family and your business removed from our neighborhood. Can you ever forgive me?" My mother's reply? "Oh heavens, that episode was a blessing in disguise! Please! Would you like to come in and have a piece of pie?" In he came, and they had a heart-to-heart over blueberry pie. That was my mom in a nutshell.

When we were scheduled to have a wake in the living room I can still hear my mom saying, "MaryBob, remember to be quiet when you come home from school this afternoon. Mr. Smith's viewing is today, and his family will be in the living room. No TV for you girls today. Just go upstairs quietly, change your clothes, then go outside and play. We'll eat dinner between visiting hours tonight." *You girls* were my friends Becky and Beth. We were inseparable and had spent our entire childhoods with each other. Becky lived up the street in front of our house, and Beth lived behind our house on another street. I was in the middle. With our strategic location, Beth and I had learned to send each other signals with our bedroom lights. "Are you home? Wanna talk on the phone?" We thought we were the perfect undercover agents. The three of us had made a habit of getting off the bus, changing clothes, grabbing a bag of chips and a pop before plunking ourselves down on the floor in front of the TV to watch "Dark Shadows." We loved every moment of those days. For us, life was sweet, and our foundation was secure. We were living in the land of milk and honey.

I remember the kindness of those families in our living room as their eyes caught me doing my best to not make noise during visitation hours. The staircase was in plain view of the open casket, and as I attempted to sneak up the steps they would say things like, "Hi" and "Don't worry about it." Such sweet people, even in their suffering. I saw them at a vulnerable time, and I sometimes thought my creeping up and down the stairs was a welcomed distraction from the sorrow at hand. It made me sad to see them so sad, and yet I rarely thought much about their loved one lying below me in a casket during the night. Looking back now, I think they knew my dad was doing the best he could for them, and they merely felt appreciative of his efforts. Accommodating for a casket in our living room was not a stretch for my parents. They never thought twice about it.

My mom did tell me once about my older brother years earlier. He was a toddler and had escaped her arms while she was giving him a bath. He ran through the living room stark naked as the family in mourning stood in front of the casket, beholding their loved one. They, of course, laughed while my poor mom, perpetually concerned about doing the right thing, cringed with embarrassment. They told my dad later that the incident provided much needed comic relief. Such was life in our house.

Deep inside I knew I was safe physically and emotionally. I knew I would always be taken care of. Our family was warm and steady. You could say that my sister and I graduated together, since she finished high school the same month that I finished kindergarten. She went off to college, so it was my brother and I at home for 3 more years. At age 9 I became the lone child in the house. It was fabulous! Let the adventures begin!

About that same time my dad and his friends decided to buy an old city bus and convert it into a mobile home for fishing trips. What started out as the craziest of ideas ended up being the coolest thing ever! And they did it all right in our driveway. I can't remember how many months it took them, but night after night they'd work on it, and it turned out to be a treasure. That bus took them far and wide to fish. They particularly loved driving to Michigan to ice fish. I'll bet the canvas on those fishing huts could tell us some tales!

Each of my parents had a tremendous sense of humor. They both smiled and laughed easily, and it was a blessing to all who knew them, particularly to us, the three kids. Lying in my bed on warm evenings I listened through my bedroom window to my dad and his friends playing horseshoes in the field behind our house. His infectious laugh rose above all the others and floated through my bedroom window as they "razzed" each other about one thing or another. Frequently about who caught the most or the biggest fish or better yet, who snored the loudest on their most recent fishing trip. Through a different bedroom window, I could see the funeral home. I suppose I had an unusual frame of reference regarding death. In retrospect, I think I had so many different frames that it was kind of a non-thing. What was a thing for me were those who mourned the person whose body was in the casket. Some survivors were traumatized and wailing. Others were relieved and laughing. Some deaths were expected, and some were premature. Families were gentle, angry, understanding, lost. It wasn't the corpse that had my attention-it was those who lived on. Sometimes at night I would turn out my light and watch the families as they left to go home, leaving their deceased loved one behind. I wondered about how they felt and how hard it was for them. I imagined the conversations they might be having and the memories they were reviewing. My dad did not discuss his business with us as he felt it would be disrespectful, so my imagination was my sole source.

Death Becomes Real

In my 14th year, two days before Christmas of my freshman year in high school I didn't have to wonder any longer. Becky, Beth and I had been planning to go Christmas caroling on that evening, the 23rd of December. It was cold, and both Beth and I had sore throats, so we weren't permitted to go. Around 9:00 p.m. the funeral home phone rang in the house. It was the local hospital asking my dad to come pick up the body of someone who had just passed away. I will never forget his hanging up the phone and whispering as he said, "Becky... DOA at St. Rita's." He put his head in his hands and wept. Our lifelong friend was gone. Hit by a car on the street while she was walking to the next house to sing. Standing in front of the pantry door I leaned my head back and slid to the floor sobbing.

For the next several nights I stared out of that same bedroom window and talked to her through the brick as if she were standing right next to me, wondering if she heard. It was Christmas so the funeral could not take place until after the 25th. We simply had to wait for the holiday to pass. Christmas that year was a *non*-Christmas. I recall Beth and I standing together staring into that casket lined in pink. There she was, our lifeless companion wearing the wrist corsage of pink roses with our two names on it. We just stood there too stunned to cry. My dad told me later that he couldn't have done what he did for a living if he had had many cases like that.

Even though Becky was no longer living in the house down the street, for months after I continued to pick up the phone to call her. Forgetting. Only to then remember and put the phone back in its cradle. To this day, I remember her phone number. It was my first experience of feeling bereft, without direction, thinking the pain would never leave me. The weeks and months wore on, and over time we all learned to laugh again, although I constantly felt her next to me. She is in my mind still, as I have passed the milestones in my life. I continue to talk to her and ask for her help when I have moments overcast by grey skies.

Death came calling again a few years later, reminding me of the sorrow I had felt at 14. A young girl in our neighborhood had died from a sudden illness. Our families were friends. I was awakened late one evening after her family had left the funeral home. The pounding that awakened me was her best friend beating her fists on the side door of our funeral home shouting Sally's name. She was doing what I had wanted to do only a few years earlier but hadn't. Her friend was sleeping inside, and she just wanted her to wake up and come outside one more time. I was witnessing her agony as my own, again.

Friday Fish and Phone Etiquette

Fish. Let's talk about fish. I think I forgot to mention that in my family Catholicism was king, so at least once a week, on Friday, fish was on our dinner plates. And let me tell you, it wasn't frozen fish sticks like we got in school. It was fresh perch that my dad had caught in some lake or reservoir. There he was, whenever possible, standing at the stove frying those little fillets and tossing them onto the paper towels before he salted them. Man! I loved that meal more than anything. Few of those fillets ever made it to the kitchen table because we ate them the minute they came out of the skillet.

My dad liked to cook, and he only pretended to get frustrated with our eating at the counter. I was proud because I had cleaned some of those fish myself. My dad had let me sit in the circle with him and his friends in the funeral home garage as they all taught me how to clean fish. The 10-year-old girl in a circle of men joking and carrying on like boys. Me with my sharp knife, smelling like fish and having the time of my life in the garage of our funeral home.

In that same garage were stored the hearse and the station wagon. If you came from a small town you'll remember that the local funeral director was likely also the area rescue squad, before there ever was such a thing. Before the days of 911 and ambulance-looking vehicles with "EMT" written on the side, my dad was that guy. One station wagon, one cot, one tank of oxygen, and one flashing red light that he could smack onto the top of the wagon when need be. The charge? $5 for an emergency call and $2 or a "say a prayer for us" for an ambulance call. Next to the hearse in the garage were stacks of folding chairs and tables. My parents rented those out for church events, parties, and any other social gathering. To help us with the funeral home and these adjunct services, our house had two different phone numbers: one for personal calls and one for business-Saint Vincent DePaul calls (more on that later).

My parents trained us well in phone etiquette and composure so as not to overreact when an emergency or death call came across the wires, and the ring-tones for the two phones were slightly different for our benefit. If the business phone was ringing we had better be composed before picking it up, AND we had better not let it ring more than three times. More than three times and the caller might think we weren't interested in having his business and reach out to another area funeral director.

Most readers of the local newspaper might scan the front page before opening it to look inside. Not so in our house. As soon as we heard the paper land on the back porch, we found the obituary section on page four. The front page could wait. We opened the paper to that page, laid it across the kitchen table, and read every word. My parents wanted to be sure the obits were typed correctly, and were endlessly concerned about those families who had chosen a different funeral home. They were forever wondering what they could have done better to help those acquaintances who did not call *us* in their grief.

I can't tell you the number of times the air got sucked right out of the room when an emergency call came in. My dad would hang up the phone and move like lightning to then fly out the back door practically airborne. No one had to say anything. The rest of us just knew to stay clear. I have one particular memory of pasting myself against the wall as my dad blew past me on his way down the stairs, throwing on his shirt and tie. There was not a more dedicated man on this earth.

Love Comes in Laughter

Although my mother was a perpetual worrier, she could find humor in the most unlikely of places. One of her favorite expressions was, "There's a lid for every pot." Whenever I heard this come out of her mouth I knew she had just laid her eyes on a couple who as individuals might not easily attract a mate. It was not mean-spirited. She had a gift for delivering commentary on the ironies in life. She was acknowledging the beauty of a world where everybody can have somebody.

My mother was a true friend, and she held strong relationships over the years with her college girlfriends who lived in town. They raised their children together, went to basketball games together, and in their later years decided it was time to give themselves a name. Due to their advanced age they elected to call themselves "The Has-Beens." Once a week they would get together to play cards and have lunch, and laugh. "Where you going, mom?" "Oh, I have a 'Has-Beens' luncheon today." Funny women. Beautiful friendships.

My mother loved hats. She had the perfect little head for a hat, and being barely five feet tall, these hats became her trademark. Unfortunately, we three kids inherited our father's head, and there's barely a hat on earth that will fit our heads. "One size fits all" is false advertising. To this day, hats sit on top of my head like a bird on a perch. Not so with my mother. Every season, every holiday she had a different hat, and we loved to see her so happy when she wore each one. Rarely did she choose one that we just couldn't appreciate. I remember an Easter hat one year that I think was one of her favorites. It was large with white and yellow daisies and a broad brim. It swallowed her up, but we never said a word. She wore it with such pride.

Over the years, although she donated most of those beloved headpieces to charity, she did hold onto her favorite favorites. They lived inside hat boxes in the cedar closet upstairs, and upon her death we decided they needed one more walk with mom. We devised a tiered hat rack and stood it next to mom's casket amongst the many flower arrangements. It held about a dozen hats. With this display, everyone could remember her style, and each hat sparked another conversation about mom and her fashion sense. She found joy in the small things, and I think that perspective saw her through more than one fearful circumstance in her long life.

My mother's laugh was self-contained. Hardly a sound escaped her lips, but the shake of her body told us everything — her mind had taken her to some place where only ripples of humor were allowed. One of my favorite memories is of my mother, almost out of breath from laughter, because of something my older brother had said. He could make us laugh like no other. In those moments, to catch her breath, she sat at the kitchen table and put her head on her arms, while her shoulders rocked with hilarity. Then she looked up and said, "Darn you, Tim. Stop it," as she cleaned her glasses and wiped her eyes. This scenario was a regular occurrence in our home, and the recollection warms me.

A classic source of family amusement were my mother's breasts. Now don't get all indignant and righteous about my making that statement. She's the one who started it, and it just took off from there. She was five foot one, and we learned later, her boobs accounted for more of her weight than we ever imagined. So, as a result, she had bra strap marks permanently engraved on her shoulders. How she ever stood up straight is beyond me. We always knew when mom had gone shopping for new "brassieres" as she called them. How? Imagine walking in the back door of your home to find four or five brassieres strapped around the chairs of the kitchen table. Yep! Mom strapped them there to stretch them out before wearing them, and they stayed there for days! Those bras and those chairs fueled our fire, and our mom was such a good sport laughing right along with us.

Allow me to recount the afternoon she enlightened us on the exact poundage of her mammary glands. I remember my sister, brother, nieces and I were sitting at the kitchen table likely discussing what to have for dinner. Around the corner came my mother with an air of authority. She looked at all of us and announced, "In case any of you, smart alecks, were wondering, I just put the bathroom scale up next to the bathroom sink and weighed my breasts. They each weigh eight pounds, and if you ever tell anyone I did this, I'll shoot you." These words flowed effortlessly from the mouth of our mother, the queen of good manners, gracious behavior, and proper social etiquette.

"What?! You did what?!" We all howled and roared 'til we cried. Nothing prepared us for this momentous occasion, and when she told us we couldn't tell anyone, we went nuts. "I mean, are you kidding us, Mom? You are, right? This is the funniest thing you've ever done, and you really think we're not going to tell anyone? Oh no, this is going straight into the Lima News (our local paper) this afternoon. No way we're keeping this quiet." We were out of control. Here's the kicker. She was in her 80s when she did that. An 82-year-old woman picked up the bathroom scale, put it on the counter and leaned over it one boob at a time to read the numbers. We insisted she demo the process for us, which sent us to the moon all over again.

In retrospect, I do believe the joy of a childhood replete with those moments so filled me up that I learned to carry the idea of humor forward as I grew. During my darker hours, when humor was not readily available, I prayed that some small detail would strike my funny bone and pull me from my depths. I remember sitting with my head in my hands, tears pouring. I sat up on the couch, determined to make my memory pull something amusing from my family's past, only to be engulfed in anger and guilt at the thought of ever having had a family at all. *What I had done to them. What they had done to me.* It would take years before I could recall those many joyful episodes without storm clouds dropping rain to wash them away in a nanosecond. It would take even longer for me to tell those stories with the essence of delight they held for all involved. Eventually, I would find that delight. I knew the energy of it was there for me to touch, but only if I got beyond myself and my own perceptions.

Combing through my past in search of joy, I remembered my father was also a jokester. I wondered at times if his growing up in a family of funeral directors, as well as being one himself, were the reasons he chose to dally with the lighter side of life. A sort of coping mechanism. Since so much of his time was spent consoling and guiding the bereaved, I believe he sought merry-making in the spaces of time he spent away from the funeral home.

Occupying one of those precious spaces was our beloved cleaning lady, Gladys. She was a frequent recipient of one of my father's favorite pranks. Looking through my young eyes I imagine Gladys was in her fifties when she became part of our family. Walking up the street from school on Fridays I would see her big green car sitting in our parking lot, and the site of it made me smile. Her bright spirit and love for all of us were precious beyond measure. For most of my childhood, Gladys shined her light on our family, and her presence was a sweet icing on our cake. The sound of her voice and the formation of her words landed in my ears as love flowing. She was who I called if I couldn't find my dance tights, and who I called when I needed straight forward down-home advice.

Before running the vacuum cleaner downstairs Gladys would plug the sweeper into the electrical socket in the bathroom then sweep the surrounding rooms. Of course, the sound of the motor running overtook the house. Perfect conditions for a sneak attack. My father — planning ahead — would come into the house through the back door, slip into that same bathroom unbeknownst to Gladys, unplug her sweeper and walk out the front door. She never saw him coming or going, but she knew who the culprit was. Her voice, raised in frustration and humor, rang through the house. "Bob Hogenkamp, you leave my sweeper alone!"

On the days he wasn't unplugging the sweeper my dad would get into Gladys' 1955 two-toned green Plymouth sitting in the funeral home parking lot. He couldn't just walk past it on his way to the funeral home. The temptation was too great. He quietly opened the driver's door and flipped every switch he could, knowing Gladys would turn the key at the end of the day. He knew full well she would jump in fright at the sound of her radio up full blast, windshield wipers flapping, and heat blowing full bore. This trick was one of his favorites.

My dad also loved to "surprise" my mom with bouquets of flowers left behind in the funeral home. You know, those flower arrangements invariably filled with red or orange gladiolas? They just scream "funeral home." I can't even count the number of times he would present them to her in any number of ways, knowing full well she was going to reject them on sight. I can still hear her say, "You take those flowers right back to where you found them. They're not staying here." At this point they would both laugh at his joke. She wanted absolutely nothing to do with these leftovers, and would make it more than clear to him, but he never gave up trying. Their love for each other and for us was sweet as honey. Warm the milk and pour some in. The perfect recipe for a good night's sleep.

ALL THAT GLITTERS

There's a lady who's sure all that glitters is gold, and she's buying the stairway to heaven – Led Zeppelin

Pagan Baby Milk Cartons

Have you ever known *somethin' just ain't right*, but everyone and everything around you was telling you it was? Yep? That was me at age seven. There I sat in my desk, the little towhead with her crooked bangs (my dad felt it his duty to control the length of my bangs), navy blue skirt, white blouse, white ankle socks, black shoes on my feet swinging above the linoleum floor. Sister Mary Evelyn stood in front of the room, wearing her black habit with rosary beads always visible, explaining to us the concept of "pagan babies."

Now I knew Sister Mary Evelyn cared for her second and third graders (we were a mixed class), but this thing she was telling us was just not hitting home with me. The Church wants us to do what? It was Lent, and I had already decided what I was going to give up for the next 40 days. It was not something I shared with anyone since, after all, I *was* seven years old. I mean, who still sucks their thumb at age seven? It was embarrassing, but my decision, though short-lived, had been made. Final.

That was when I learned about the Catholic missionaries in Africa. Missionaries in Africa? Why in heaven's name were we all the way over in Africa? And doing what? My child's mind was trying to wrap itself around the idea that we were trying to get the Africans to believe as we did. I kept thinking, "Don't they have their own ideas about God? Aren't they doing just fine the way they are?" Sister Mary Evelyn explained to us that the Diocese of Toledo had given each of us a milk carton to take home, fill with coins and send to Africa for a "pagan baby." We had the option of naming our baby, if we wanted, as that might help bring us a sense of closeness to those we were helping.

At the end of Lent, we were to return the filled cartons, and the Church would use the funds to help the African babies who needed us. Our collections would help buy food and clothing for our "babies," even though I had yet to determine what exactly "Pagan" meant. I learned years later that the kids at another Catholic elementary school in town received statues of the Blessed Virgin Mary for this same purpose. Their statues had a coin slot in the back for donations. At our school, it was milk cartons.

Now I'd like to mention here that I was all in for the "giving and helping people with food and clothing" part. And the Catholic Church was all about giving. What I just could not get a grip on was the "Our missionaries will teach them about the Catholic faith" part. Why? Why don't we just call it a day after distributing the food and stuff? I glanced at my friends sitting around me, and it looked like they were swallowing this idea hook, line, and sinker. I'm fairly certain that for the remainder of that day I was not paying attention in class because when I got home I pretty much ran through the house to find my mom in the kitchen.

"Mom! Look what they gave us in school today," handing her the milk carton. "Sister Mary Evelyn says we're supposed to put our quarters and stuff in it during Lent so that we can send the money to the missionaries in Africa. For the pagan babies." I'm sure my mother nodded her head in agreement, so I kept on.

"What's a pagan baby anyway?"

No doubt she smiled and explained to me that a pagan was someone who worshipped false gods, *not because they were bad people*, they just hadn't had the opportunity to know our one true God, so that's why our priests were there to tell them about Him.

"Mom, that's stupid!" at which point she would have given me a look because "stupid" was a bad word in our house.

"OK, not stupid. But I don't get it. Why don't we just send money for stuff like food and medicine? Why do we gotta send priests over there to talk to them about being Catholic? Why don't we just leave that part out and help them with the other stuff? I mean, they can believe what they want, right? Why do we gotta do that?! I don't like it, and I'm not putting any of my change in that dumb carton!"

My mom told me then and every Lent for the next six years the same thing. Basically, it was some version of, "As Catholics we think it's beneficial for people to hear what we believe since they probably have not had the chance to know our God." Every Lent thereafter I argued my anti-missionary point, even into adulthood. "So, if we collect quarters in milk cartons, they get to go to heaven?"

This was an occasion when I felt a tear in the fabric of my perfect little world, and it was not to be the last. My little seven-year-old brain and heart just said, "no," to that milk carton, and with that one word I believe I planted a seed of curiosity and challenge that would stay with me for a long time. No one was ever going to convince me that it was good for everyone to believe the same thing. Even at seven I had learned just enough about other exciting people and places that it seemed there was room for more than one perspective. I wanted to know all of them, just to know them, for myself, to soak in their ways of living in the world. If everyone had the same ideas, there would be nothing new to experience. How completely boring!

The World Outside of Pleasantville

Fortunately, being the youngest in the family, I was the beneficiary of my parent's improving financial situation. My older siblings never failed to remind me that their vacations were spent at nearby Indian Lake, while I got to go to Paris. My eternal response? "I can't help it you were born ten years too soon." My parents had a compassion and curiosity of their own. My dad eventually convinced my mom to travel in an airplane, so at ten I went with them to NYC. I thought I was looking pretty sharp in my olive-green skirt and sweater vest. No one would ever know I was just a country mouse in the big city. I was agog as we walked the streets of the Bowery in Manhattan. I had never seen men sleeping and eating on the sidewalks. I wasn't frightened, *but I was curious.* I wanted answers to my questions. Thank God, my parents were accepting of my boundless energy and need for explanations.

At thirteen I found myself in Guatemala. My brother, who had joined the Peace Corps, had proposed to his Guatemalan girlfriend, so mom and dad decided to go meet our new family. I, of course, was allowed to go too. Stepping off that plane in Latin America was a steroid shot to my desire to experience all things different. I took it all in with every breath. The soldiers standing on the street corners with their machine guns ready were probably the biggest shock along with the children begging in the streets.

There had been political unrest at that time, so for those soldiers to see us while we traveled, it was mandatory for us to keep the dome lights on inside our car. Unlike the shock of seeing homeless people sleeping on the streets in NYC, this was a bodily-felt shock that danger was afoot. Why the need for such protection? I wanted to know more. The children in the streets? Through my young eyes it appeared as if no one even noticed them. They were invisible. The explanations I was given failed to satisfy my need to understand how the local adults could pretend those kids weren't there tugging on their shirts. My parents were ready to give at every turn.

Despite the challenges there, if you ever get the chance to experience Christmas or Easter in Latin America, take it! That culture puts us to shame when it comes to celebrations! Firecrackers were laid along the city streets on Christmas Eve, and at midnight the explosions were both deafening and exhilarating. The city was afire with light and sound. My world burst free, and I was in love with life. Never had I witnessed such collective, unharnessed glee. Everyone everywhere was celebrating. If an "engagement meter" had been placed on each of my five senses, the readings would have been off the charts. The lights, sounds, smells, textures, and tastes of Latin America entered my system that night and stayed a lifetime. What had previously been a passing interest in all things "different" was blown wide open as the water rushing down a mountain after the melting of winter snow. I wanted to experience more. To see more. To understand more. To live more. I believe in that moment the idea of my following the road of a picket fence and paneled station wagon went right out the window. Who were these people? What was their history? What influences affected their way of life? How could so many be so poor and yet so filled with joy? The trajectory of my life was set then and there. I didn't recognize it at the time, of course. Years later, peering back, I would appreciate the impact of that trip. As Steve Jobs once said, "We can't connect the dots (of our lives) looking forward. We can only connect them looking back." My trips to Guatemala were, at that point, the largest of dots in my life.

The next day we went to the Mayan market at Chichicastenango. What a world of color! The vendors we saw there wrapped in their beautifully woven shawls and shirts so struck me that I'm sure I stood staring and smiling at them, unaware that I had stopped walking. My heart instantly opened to all things indigenous. Delighted. That's the word. I was delighted at every turn. Who were these people? What were they thinking? How did they live when they weren't in the market? What did their houses look like? What did they believe? The colors and music spun around me. Their dark eyes shone with intensity, and I was hypnotized. The questions in my head were endless, and the idea of finding answers invigorating. Oh, wait. Hold up. Let's not forget the meat market. Not so "delighted" there. Whoa, Nelly, my olfactory nerve got a jolt, the extent of which I will never forget. It might have been the first time I ever considered becoming vegetarian, if I even knew that word then.

I began to feel perhaps I really did grow up in a bubble, that my Norman Rockwell picture of reality was being infiltrated by the other realities of the world. And then more questions began to arise. Why so many poor people everywhere? Why the soldiers and their guns? Why the servants in the house when the wife didn't even have a job? Remember, I had a mother who worked outside the home as teacher, inside the home as wife and mother, and in the family business as business partner, makeup artist and hair stylist. My paradigms were clashing, but the collision was invigorating.

That trip still affects me today. It was there that I made the decision to learn to speak Spanish. Admiring my brother's ability to communicate with our new friends, I determined, then and there, that I would master their language someday. Visiting Latin America quite literally set me on my life's path. My parents agreed with my decision to study Spanish in high school and study abroad in college. As a result, I became a high school Spanish teacher and led multiple student tours to Europe and Latin America. I wanted my "kids" to feel the same wonder I had felt upon witnessing other approaches to life. Exposing others to new ways of seeing the world became a passion I've not outgrown. It was there I learned to not judge a book by its cover. It was later in my study abroad I learned stereotypes are nothing more than convenient boxes to contain what we refuse to understand. They may occasionally be amusing, but they are formed of ignorance.

Returning from Guatemala, we flew back to Ohio landing in Cincinnati. As we touched down the airplane skidded on ice and slid off the runway, landing in the grass. It was unsettling, to say the least. I have sometimes wondered if that incident was a metaphor for my attempts at staying between the rails of "normal" societal rules. I've always landed, but it hasn't always been according to the books. For more reasons than I can delineate here, and despite the lack of luster in some spots, I was head over heels enchanted with life. For the most part that feeling stayed with me through the next twenty years of ups and downs, until one day it packed its bags and took a lengthy sabbatical. I had hints along the way that something might be amiss, but I was ill-prepared for the near-fatal tidal wave headed my way.

The Defiance-Guilt Loop

The first layer of glitter fell from my gilded world with my being matriculated into the world of guilt and patriarchy. Guilt is the gift that keeps on giving, and the bestowers, either wittingly or unwittingly, are many; parents, religious institutions, judicial systems, and the beat goes on. Patriarchy? Wow. The source of that thinking is ancient and broad. For centuries this concept was both theological and social. Remember Henry VIII? Now there's some patriarchy for you! Somewhere along the way, listening and observing, I picked up an attitude that went something like, "If you're not female, don't tell me what to do! About anything! Don't tell me how to start the grill. Don't tell me what I should think. And you'd better not tell me what you think I did wrong. Just stay in your business, and out of my mine."

No anger there, right? Where did all the heat behind those little gems come from? My best explanations to myself have gone something like, "Well, the Catholic Church held all the cards during my childhood." Remember here, I'm not blaming. I'm excavating. See my shovel? It was, after all, the Sixties. Women were not on the altar, behind the screen in the confessional or named "Pastor" of any church. The news broadcasts were all about men in power. Misogyny as a result of outspoken females was like a dark thriller. Nerve-wracking and spellbinding. We had all read about Henry's six powerless wives, and only occasionally would a woman roll through our textbooks as a heroine, only to die as a martyr for some cause. Of the hundreds of images looking up from those pages, few were women.

At that time in my life the concept of *power with* had not occurred to me. Women were shouting across the nation for recognition, and *power over* men seemed the only way to get it. It was everywhere, except in our little town. As I recall, nothing much changed. The most I saw the women do at the time was raise their eyebrows at the news broadcasts and continue cooking dinner. Most of that time my potential ball of fire was contained at room temperature in a well-ventilated area. When the air got stuffy or the temp went up, it was ignition and blast off. I later gave that particular pattern of anger a label. I called it the "Defiance-Guilt Loop." Defiance because it was the only way I knew to shape my disagreement with someone, and guilt because invariably, after the detonation I would slink back to my "Good Girl" chair and carry on as ever. Get ready for a classic example.

Our school was a couple of miles from home, and on warm days my friends and I walked home from school, stopping at the nearby pharmacy for something to eat and drink. Standing behind the glass on a raised dais was an *always happy* pharmacist who would greet us by name and make jokes with us as we grazed the candy aisle. We knew he liked us, and of course, we liked him right back. He let us call him by his first name, which made us feel extra important. Little did I suspect, that same jovial man would someday be my loving father-in-law. With what I knew of him over the years, the following came as a bit of a shock.

"The women in our family don't sit down at the dinner table until the men have been given their plates of food first," I heard my future father-in-law say to me. He, the father of four boys and five girls, a first-generation American of Hungarian heritage, was seated at the head of the large empty dining room table. His wife, my future mother-in-law, was busy getting the Sunday supper ready for the 14 members of this glorious family. She had just shooed me out of the kitchen to go get my piece of chicken from the grill. Their oldest son, my fiancé, was in charge of the cooking outside.

They were his words, his tradition, and I was stunned. He had stopped me in my tracks. Another male figure in my life giving me a directive. He wasn't the local priest or teacher, or my own brother. I went silent like a scolded child. The air conditioner humming was the only sound. Twenty-six years old, and having known this affable man from a distance my entire life, I was struck dumb. I knew he had certain expectations of his wife and children, but nothing so blatantly chauvinistic as this. He was dead serious, and inside I began feeling a not-so-very-slow boil rising to the occasion.

My family household was very nearly the flip side of this. My grandmother, the 23-year-old widowed mother of three, came from a family of strong equitable men and women, her mother-in-law having been the first female bank owner in the state of Ohio. Although the paternalistic influences of mid-century society were felt in my home, servitude was not one of them. If anything, my father was protective, and slightly resentful of my mother's education and authority. Nobody ever told her what to do. Theirs was an egalitarian, maybe somewhat female-leaning, relationship.

My eyes stared at the grilled chicken breast on my plate, and this is what fell out of my ungracious mouth; "Well, in my family the men have arms and legs just like the women, so they can go get their own food." My defiance chomping at the bit. The air was thick and silent between us. Eating out of the question. A few minutes of that and I slid my chair back, stood, strode from the room, and left my full plate next to the lone man sitting in the dining room.

By the time I reached my fiancé standing at the grill in the back yard I was blurting expletives that did not help my case any. "Your dad is…. and you better *never* act like that toward me! I am not his…. servant or yours! What your mom allows is her shit, but I will *not* bow down to either one of you." I was clearly having a moment.

In all honesty, I have no recollection of his reaction to my tirade. All I remember is eventually, we went back into the house. This time I sat at the kitchen table instead (there were always two tables-full due to the number of family members), my future father-in-law patting my shoulder as he passed behind me. I think now that he understood me more than I did him. By that time, I was beginning the fall into guilt. Guilt for having disrespected him and guilt for using my juiciest foul language to describe him. Oh, and let's not forget guilt for making demands on my fiancé. My as-of-yet-unrecognized pattern of defiance and guilt, particularly with men, had reared its head. It would take me another twenty years to recognize this repeated pattern and give it its very own name.

If I had drawn a flow chart, the overarching title would have been "Accept What I'm Being Fed For the Sake of Peace," followed by "Tamp Down My Own Views," "Live in Compliance," "Enjoy the Good Times," "Recognize the Rise of Resentment," "Choose to Rock the Boat or Remain Silent," "Begin Countdown to Ignition," "Lift off," "Drop Rocket Booster," "Lick My Wounds," "Return to Home Base," "Maintain Holding Pattern 'til Next Time."

As I look back at myself and watch others in the same loop I wonder where the pattern began. Simplified, I believe I heard, "God loves you more than anything, but even He has his limits. This game of 'free will' you're playing, mixed with a dash of 'It's God's will' is all a big crap shoot. In the end He, because we know 'She' was not appropriate, will decide your fate, so if you mess it up, you'd better be contrite enough to gain His mercy before you leave this planet. Otherwise your feet are gonna get mighty hot."

These attempts to control were couched in the cloak of love and obedience. "The Lord decrees," or "The Church requires." It felt as if there was a rule for everything. Do this. Don't do that. You have a mind, but be sure to use it for the right things. You have the power to decide, but be sure to decide according to what we're telling you. You have free will, but here's the guidebook. Where in heaven's name was there room for trial and error? The rumblings of "women's lib" were just getting noticed, adding fuel to a smoldering fire. It seemed that to be heard, we had to be angry. Then when we appeared angry, we were perceived as being disrespectful. Then to atone for our disrespect, we had to be repentant (guilty). There had to be a better way to move toward strength and self-determination without having to shout. This road was filled with land mines, just waiting to be stepped on.

The Conundrum of Obedience

The one male voice I was willing to hear was that of my father. Of his love, I had no doubt. Should any other male *suggest* or *recommend* I do something, I would rear up, feeling manipulated and tamped down. It was as if I could see a whip being used to control me. Any directive from my older brother or from the parish priest caused my little eyes to squint. At times I felt confusion that God actually punished people. I had heard He was all-loving. How did those two ideas go together? I wondered how I could feel right about something and yet judged as wrong by God. It can be crazy-making when you judge your own feelings in an attempt to succumb to a belief from outside of yourself. Simple example? A hamburger sounded mighty good after a Friday night football game, but no meat on Fridays for us Catholics. Who made up that rule?

The nuns, of course, were our teachers, but it was clear where the power lay. The priests were the pastors of the church. They heard our confessions and dispensed our penance. They were on the altar saying Mass, and when they stepped into our classrooms, it was a special event. Once again, many of these men were honorable, kind, and caring. We felt "chosen" when given their attention. It just felt imbalanced, even then, patronizing, controlling, in the name of tradition. To me it was most apparent when the Bishop of the diocese showed up. Lots of men in fancy robes and the bishop wearing his miter. The irony for me was that I dearly loved the orthodox rituals. Loved the music, the ceremony, the garb. I felt entranced by the pageantry, and when I witness this now, it gives me goosebumps so high you could hang shirts on them.

Those traditions are an enigma to me. Part of me wants to shout, "Give a woman your tall hat! Allow some feminine energy on that altar and see what happens!" The other part of me wants to sit in awe and wonder, as I did in my childhood, soaking up centuries of liturgy and ceremony, quizzing myself on the correct terminology for each ceremonial piece.

Childhood and young adulthood had passed. Being told what to do and doing just that was both a survival mechanism and a gift to myself, feeling the warmth of approval shower over me from my parents, teachers, and parish priests. The choices I made felt like the right things to do, and I think they were. As an observer, I could see myself making many "right" and traditionally expected choices, but in my head, I was occasionally dreaming of the freedom felt by those who marched to the beat of their own drummer. The dream was uncomfortable and more like that guest or that fish that smells after three days, it made me squirm. I felt compromised somehow. I sloughed it off, wanting it to leave me alone.

Some of those whom I secretly admired were local and others widely known. I admired people that lived their truth. That didn't wait for everyone's approval. They appeared to be fearless, although I'm sure they weren't. The founder of our local high school was one of those. He was a small man with a huge impact on the world around him. Msgr. E. C. Herr was a force of nature, and most held strong opinions about him. The word "waver" did not exist for him. Some loudly disagreed with him. I adored him for his independent spirit and determination to guide those who were aimless. He was both tough and soft-hearted, direct and compassionate. He was at once a task master and a safe haven. He lived his life full out.

Others were names and stories that crossed my path and left me wondering how they managed to do what they did. Mother Teresa, Karen Blixen (Out of Africa), Rigoberto Menchu (Nobel laureate). None of these humans were perfect, yet their fortitude and indomitability were, in my eyes, exemplary. They had an impact on the world. They spent their time on this earth living passionately, foregoing what might have been an easier existence.

In the middle of basking in my beautiful life I longed for that kind of freedom, but felt loyalty and the need for approval simultaneously. I suspect I was not alone in this compromise. As I grew into myself the demand for certain behaviors began to grate on me just a bit, and although I outwardly conceded, my inner defiant voice was secretly sharpening its tone, readying for the perfect opportunity for rebuttal.

Once voiced, that rebuttal, was either accepted and allowed or squashed as an example of disrespect and lack of gratitude. If squashed, was this where self-doubt entered? I recall asking myself the question, "Is this all there is? Will the rest of my days be spent playing this same record over and over?" I'm not saying it was a bad record, and therein lay the conflict. I had so much yet couldn't see my future self, living out my days where I was. I had forced myself to look ahead to my future me, and although I wasn't sure where I did see myself, I was sure where I didn't. All the love and tradition from the outside could not hold me, and the internal clamoring was deafening. Was I being ungrateful? Selfish? A complete and total brat? Who the hell thinks like this? Why can't I just be satisfied? Why the need for something different? I'm choking on all the damned rules. I think I might be losing it. Anybody in my shoes would stick it out and keep their mouth shut. If I don't know what it is I *do* want, then how in the heck can I say I *don't* want what I already have? Maybe if I pray more. Go to Mass more. Maybe God will give me an answer. I know I shouldn't be thinking like this. I'm not being appreciative enough. Mom says, God says, the Church says. How can I even get past all those voices to find my own? The ping-pong match inside my head was exhausting, and the crowd was getting agitated.

What happens the moment we begin to believe that someone else's opinion is more valuable than our own? That they're right, and we're wrong? I'm talking about that nagging voice that keeps telling us one thing or another. It seemed at the time that many women tolerated male dominance. Quietly. Even now we live in societies where women with a voice are viewed as a threat and are then labeled. Yes, the balance is evening out, but a universal recognition of each individual's value still eludes many of our cultures. Gender may or may not be the determining factor, and I believe some men feel an equal, but opposing sense of pressure that has been passed down through the years to them. I wonder if some men would prefer to *not* be the holders of the crown.

This societal acceptance is subtle at times. Women in relationship may still seek permission to buy this, go here, make a change, and if that permission is not freely granted may fall into defiance. It's a fine line between respecting our partners and feeling the need to ask for their approval. One is voluntary and life giving. The other is a result of feeling "not good enough." The never-ending search for approval can bind our gifts and suppress our spirits.

Does repeated self-doubt lead us to more episodes of defiant behavior? Those moments when we simply refuse to allow another to have any influence over our thoughts or actions? Are we fed up with being told what to think or do, so we burst like a balloon with too much air? I am certain that had I been born fifty years earlier, I would have been a street-marching suffragette. As it was I held onto the "good girl" image while secretly entertaining the visions of a "Libber." It was not a conscious plotting to overthrow. I'm pretty sure I wasn't even aware of what was burning until the flames got out of control.

Where does guilt find itself in this? Standing behind us whispering in our ear, "Who do you think you are anyway?" Once disobedient or disrespectful we — girls in particular —must seek forgiveness in order to ease our way back into a peaceful existence. Forgiveness requires a guilty party in conventional thought. That's us. Once forgiven we can tiptoe our way back into our previous lives until the next time, guilt following us like an autumn shadow. We can look the other way, but it's still stuck to our shoes.

How to stop the loop? Or at least slow its frequency? I believe we begin by being gentle with ourselves. Taking the time to acknowledge our strengths and vulnerabilities. Witnessing our own emotional responses. Acknowledging our intrinsic value as a spiritual being. Really spending the mental and emotional energy to examine why we feel the need to get angry when another imposes his/her opinion on us. For me, I believe the "why" was the heavy hand of a paternalistic church. It was a place in time where that approach made sense to most. I believed that to be heard I, as a female, had to be outwardly defiant, then recoil to save myself from myself, from my own hot flare. Once I recognized my own thought process, years later, of course, most of the fizz went out of that bottle of soda. Over time I learned to notice me when emotions rose to the surface. I now get caught in the loop less frequently and with far less intensity.

When I do find myself in the defiance-guilt loop, I remember now to stop and look inside. If I can hear my own voice I can stop playing victim to another who may not be hearing me. As long as I believe my own emotions are dependent on someone else's response to me, I can never live my life in full expression. Recognition is one thing. Blame quite another. It does nothing for me to blame the players in my story. Nothing can change the past, yet the recognition of how I interpreted the behavior of others can open the door to a more satisfying future. I now choose to believe those early voices of control came from sincerity, not malice, in most cases. There may have been, of course, those who enjoyed pounding the gavel in judgement. Humans are a funny lot. The relief of recognizing "that was then, and this is now" is life giving. I can only live now.

Thinking Outside of the Confession Box

I know as an adult I found it difficult to be kind to myself. I thought I could have/should have done something differently in the past. I thought I ought to have known better, been smarter, payed more attention, chosen more wisely, and on and on. And it can still show up during my days at work and at home, if I'm not vigilant. I could have done this or that. Maybe I'm not smart enough, young enough or assertive enough. Why am I so nice to others and so mean to me?"

I have a theory, and although my particular version belongs to me, I think you may see some of you in it. Ok, so here we go. Swirled through the layers of my ever-so-delectable childhood was the practice of going to confession. If you're familiar with this idea, you may/may not agree with my take on it. Life is all about perception, right? If you've no idea what confession is all about, then allow me to give you my brief, exclusive version.

Remember the little girl listening to the "pagan baby" explanation? The one whose feet did not yet reach the linoleum beneath her chair? Well, that was grade two. Take it all back a year to grade one. At that point, uneven bangs were not an issue. Keeping my hair combed at all was. Our teacher was Sister Mary Judith, a small tender-hearted young woman. I don't think her feet reached the floor either, by the way. She was the one who laid the groundwork for our First Confession. Recalling that term makes my eyes flutter. First Confession? Like the first of multitudes?

I don't recall the justification exactly, but the idea was clear. We were all born sinners, and although our Original Sin had been erased at baptism, humans still sinned on a regular basis. In our belief system, going to confession was the reprieve from punishment we would get from God if our sins were not confessed. Talking to God directly about our wrongdoings was not enough to "clean our slates." We had to speak to a priest. Not a nun. No reprieves.

Well, let me tell you, I didn't like the idea one bit, but somehow that sweet nun convinced me — as I'm sure she was convinced — that we were born with sin, lived our lives as sinners, and needed a priest to confess to. My little ears heard it and absorbed it like a beach towel in the pool. Yep! That was me! The six-year-old sinner! Up 'til now the worst part of my sunny life had been a scabbed knee. Now this! Me, born with Original Sin, that black mark on my tiny soul that I didn't even put there! Eve! What the heck were you thinking? And I had been having so much fun climbing trees and playing kick-the-can. Wow... the glitter fell like rain. So, ok, what now? Confession comes to the rescue.

Every Friday we formed a single-file line and marched our mini-selves from the school building across the black-top to the church for our turn in the confessional. We were trained to listen for our teacher's clicker. One click, genuflect, two clicks, file into the appropriate pew and kneel. Classmates and I still laugh at that whole concept! The confessional itself was a dark box with a mysterious screen between me and the priest. Dark enough so he wouldn't know who I was. Or so I thought. In the pews we kneeled beforehand, contemplating our own behavior over the previous week. Hands folded in prayer, heads bowed, mine with a white lace chapel cap bobby-pinned firmly to my hair. A head covering in church was required for females only, not males.

As much as I believed all of what I was taught, here I felt challenged most of the time. The option of going in to that box with nothing to confess was very simply not an option at all. I couldn't go in there and say, "Father, this past week I was perfect. No sins to report here. I'll catch you next time." I just had to think of something to say. I'm quite sure I wasn't perfect, but this process of daily analysis of my sinful behavior was the birth of a lifelong habit, one I have spent the past decades attempting to unlearn. So, the answer? What else? I invented sins to confess, so I could be like everyone else. I lied (a sin) to the priest to fulfill my weekly quota of confessable sins. Is that jacked up or what?!

Let me give you my top 3:

A. "I talked back to my parents." Trust me, talking back to my parents was *not* something that I did. Are you kidding me? As loving as my parents were, I'm relatively certain the consequences of "back talking" would not have been pleasant. I shiver at the thought.

B. "I lied." Now this one may have had a tinge of potentiality. It was quite possible that when asked about the origin of the beautiful lilacs I presented for the Blessed Virgin's May altar, I may have said, "My yard." Anyone who lived in my neighborhood knew there was not a lilac bush in our yard, but I was sure the lady down the street wouldn't miss a few blooms, right?"

C. "I was unkind to my neighbor." Another potentially true statement. No doubt, with the number of kids in our neighborhood, and the roughhousing we did, I could have said or done something "un-Christ like." Maybe.

Beth and I, to this day, can still recall discussing which sins to confess in a given week. There we were with Becky, standing on the playground in our boots and mittens, deciding which sins would get the least amount of penance. If we said we disobeyed our parents, that was sure to get a load of Apostle Creeds. That prayer took way too long to say, so we tried to steer clear when possible by saying, "I disrespected my teacher" or "I was mean to a friend." That got us a Lord's

Prayer and an Act of Contrition. Yep! Let's go that route! We could knock those prayers out in a jiffy, be out the door and back on the playground in no time! Deal!

There's a certain humor in the telling of that story, but I believe it was the beginning of a grey area in my mind. We were being taught *right* from *wrong*, but was I manipulating the system to satisfy my judges, and as a result giving away my own power to appear *acceptable* in their eyes? I still had this nagging feeling. Where was the truth and where was the lie? And whose truth was it anyway? Maybe this is where I began to betray myself and depend on the truth of others to determine my own value. I was *good* as long as others saw me that way. If I perceived *you're wrong or bad* from those around me I recoiled into myself and went to guilt for not being more of what they expected. What did I know anyway? They seemed to know a *sin* or a wrong turn when they saw one, so their opinion mattered most.

This dynamic was particularly apparent between my mother and me. Let me relate to you a couple of examples, but first know this; The incredible power of my mother's words to sway my behavior was unknown, even to her. In her later years she said to me, "I never recognized my power over you. If I had, I would have been more careful with what I said to you." I so adored and respected her, I held onto her every word, facial expression, and opinion. The last thing in the world I wanted to do was, in any way, disappoint her or my dad.

I was a good student in school, and I learned early on how much I loved people of all kinds. I loved their stories, their ideas, their jokes. It's still true today, and I'm proud of that personal characteristic, but as a result I talked a lot in class. The combination of good grades and lots of talk produced report cards with low scores in *conduct*. Invariably I'd bring home a grade card with As and Bs in everything but conduct, one teacher commenting, "No matter where I put her in the room, she makes friends." I had obviously not yet learned to flip off my *chat switch*. My mom was NOT one bit happy with that comment. I remember her standing over me, grade card in hand, as I sat on the edge of the couch. My dad had just given me a hug and walked out the back door-his great escape. My mother started in with, "This is not *my* report card. This is *yours*, and it will follow you for the rest of your academic career. It's on *your* permanent record, and I doubt that any college admissions officer will appreciate your lack of respect. To say that I am disappointed would be an understatement."

Years later my mother found an essay I had written shortly after her *conduct* speech that day. In it, I declared I would rather have been slapped in the face than "guilted" into behaving. That way I could have been angry at *her* instead of at *me*. We both laughed at the discovery of that essay, but I meant what I wrote. The guilt I felt ate at me for a long time. My conduct grades improved, at least for the time being.

The fear of feeling guilty plagued me for most of my life. That horrible sensation deep in my solar plexus could lead me to despair, and I did everything in my power to avoid any behavior that might result in my feeling guilty. If I sensed that what I was doing might result in someone else, particularly my mother, perceiving me as being *bad*, I ran as fast as I could the other way. Rarely did I allow myself to go too far down any road if I sniffed potential repercussions in the air. I was scared to death of what others might think about me because then I would have to agree with them. The guilt for not living up to their standards would kill me.

Allow me to recount one of my more profound *exceptions* — a classic case of what some might view as *good girl falls for bad boy*.

Paul sat behind me in Sister Marilyn's English class, and although I had heard he had some interesting extra-curricular activities, I thought he was so damned cute! We wore uniforms to school every day, but I would see him occasionally at some weekend event with his long hair (remember 1970?), tie dyed shirts, cut-off jeans, and dog chain around his neck — not exactly what my parents had in mind for me. Being the *talker* I was, we eventually became friends and then more. The problem was that before *more*, me and my big mouth had already been spilling the beans about him to my parents, telling them about all of his weed-smoking, rock-band-groupie experiences. When I later delicately laid out the idea of dating him, the answer was a firm, "No." What's a girl to do?

Let's see, if I added just a few miles to my trip to the grocery store I could stop by his house on my way home. The Friday night ball games were another great opportunity for a meetup, not to mention the school dances afterward. We weren't doing anything wrong, and my parents would never know the difference, right? Gotta love a close-knit community like ours. Our little rendezvous went on for a few months until a "concerned friend" felt the need to send an anonymous, cut-out-creepy-text-ransom-like letter, to my parents. Oh boy!

I was unaware of the impending onslaught of guilt as I bounced in the back door that day after school, expecting to find my mom in the kitchen like usual. She wasn't there. I shouted for her, but no answer. As I headed for the stairs my eyes landed on her sorrowful face. She was sitting alone in the rarely-used living room with a piece of paper in her hand. As I approached her asking what was wrong, she handed me the letter. I read the letter, and can't begin to describe to you the pain that shot through my body.

"Read this and weep."
"We trusted you."
"We believed in you."
"We loved you."
"We counted on you, and you betrayed us. How could you?"

The scar from that experience took years to heal. I had made my bed, and I got to lie in it. The guilt was infinite. It swallowed me up. Of course, once again, I turned it inward and found every reason in the world to hate myself for causing my parents pain. Outwardly my anger was pointed at the one who sent the letter, but in my heart, I blamed myself.

The sorrow of that experience lasted a few months until one day Paul decided to make an appointment with my dad. He asked to meet with him in his funeral home office. He explained his intentions and promised to take good care of me, to not put me in harm's way. My dad trusted Paul's heart, and today, decades later, Paul and I are the dearest of friends. He still tells me of the profound effect my father had on his life. The trust my dad had in him and the generosity my dad showed others still deeply impact Paul's own choices as an adult.

Incidents like that, along with learning the skill of tabulating my personal transgressions on a weekly basis for confession, I believe, laid the groundwork for a life of self-judgment and guilt. I became adept at giving others a "pass" on their behavior, but rarely allowed myself the same privilege. The bar I set for myself was perpetually just beyond reach, and my grasping and missing resulted in more than a few episodes of self-denigration. I learned to expect nothing less than general perfection from myself. Yes, it was motivating, but I could exhaust myself as well. I suspect that those around me suffered as much as I did during my periods of not feeling good enough. Have you ever noticed that when you're upset with yourself you aren't quite as "cuddly" to those around you? I have. Poor babies.

Looking back now as if I were an observer, I see that there was a strong element of "Don't tell me what to do!" running in my veins. I've tried to determine why, but have not come up with an answer. I just *really* didn't like being told what to do or not do. I suppose nobody does. As I got older, it seemed to get worse. Don't tell me what to think. Don't tell me how to feel. Don't tell me that I was born a sinner, and an all-loving God would choose to send me to Hell because I decide to use the free will He supposedly gave me in the first place. Just don't! I'm pretty sure that particular sentiment showed itself early on, and I'm pretty sure the logs for that fire were laid inside the confessional.

Full of Should

"I should have done that differently. You should have called me! She should know better. We should have paid more attention. He should have done better on that test." I was living on a heap of stinking should. If at least one of those sentences doesn't ring a bell with you, I'll be shocked. I spent more than a few moments a day "shoulding" the world and everyone in it, particularly myself. Feel free to interchange "should" with "need to." It's the same thing. Just for the heck of it, I tried counting the number of times I used "should" or "need to" in a given day. Unless I waited until bedtime to start counting I had double digits before lunch! I had to stay wide awake all day to do this, and was stunned at myself in the end.

I recognized I hadn't been hearing myself because I was so convinced that my own perspective was right. I just couldn't imagine there being another way. I mean, don't you *agree* that Aunt Edna "should" have given her favorite niece more than $50 for a wedding gift? Talk about cheap! And on and on it goes. I was rarely without an opinion about what someone else should or should not have done, including myself. I also realized that many of the "shoulds" were inaudible, playing inside my head.

For a case in point I'm going to give you my own most recent dalliance into the world of "shoulds." Although this topic has been on my mind for quite a while, and I am usually aware of my own usage, it was only two days ago that I decided it was time to get it off my chest and write about it. I very intentionally sat down on my favorite chair on the back porch and began the first sentence.

Let's do a little "aside" here to set the scene. Ok, I've been writing ideas like this for years, thinking that one day these ideas might amount to something that could potentially help others who are looking for a different perspective. Little things here and there that just might turn into big ways of handling the passages of life differently. My beloved coworkers hear me day in and day out spouting what they have now termed "MaryBobisms," and I've dreamed of a broader audience. A book! Of course! I could see if one day before I take the "Big Trip" I could find someone who liked my stuff and would publish it. Yes! What a great darned idea! Let's do that.

Ok, here we go. Years have passed, right? Now I find myself in the thrilling position of having a conversation with a potential editor. Am I jazzed or what? I have been checking my email 40 times a day for the past week and nothing. I'm not discouraged, just eager. Maybe it was the hurricane that caused the delay. Maybe the editor is just really busy.

Keep dreaming the dream, MaryBob. It will come when the time is right.

Back to my favorite chair. I write the first couple of sentences and something tells me to check my email again on my phone. Only this time I used the little search box to search the editor's name. Voilà! There he is! Yes! He wrote me an email! Then I read the date of his email and see that he had sent it a week ago. A week ago!? What!?!?! I missed it? How can that be? I've been staring at this inbox for days! There is no way! Ugh!! He probably thinks I just don't care and is on to the next person. Get ready, 'cuz here it comes…. I "should" have been checking that search box all along. Damn! My self-judgement kicks in, and off I go!

As I mentioned earlier, I've been aware of the word "should" for many years now, and as soon as I heard myself say it to myself I pressed my two lips together to shut myself up, and here's why:

Any way you twist it, "shoulding" someone, including ourselves, is a form of judgment. A former teacher of mine used to say that "judgment causes at least one of three things; pain, conflict, or abuse." I believed him then, and I believe him now.

Think on that one for a minute because it matters to you and to everyone in your life. Think of one time you did or didn't do something you thought you "should" have. Maybe you could have been more understanding with someone. Maybe you didn't speak up in defense of someone else. Maybe you lied or cheated or laughed. There are thousands of ways we can disappoint ourselves. The kicker is that our disappointment in ourselves may come across as anger or judgement of another. Right? I get angry at myself and to make myself feel better I'm gonna find something about *you* that really pisses me off! I'm going to point my finger at someone else. That takes the heat off me ... supposedly. And that, my dear friends, is a habit that can be unlearned.

Pick up the glitter that has fallen off you and sprinkle it all over yourself again! The more you seek a profound love of *you*, the better this world will be for not only you. Those around you will feel the difference too.

GLASS HOUSES

"What of the old serpent who cannot shed his skin, and calls all others naked and shameless?"
– Khalil Gibran

The Paradox of Compassionate Judgment

You know one of the best parts of living in a tight Catholic community? Friday and Saturday night sports! There is nothing like it anywhere. It's a virtual lovefest filled with good people laughing and carrying on as if they don't have a worry in the world. It's a reprieve from the world of work, an opportunity to sit and visit, scream and shout, all for the home team. It's slaps on the back, tears on the cheeks, and camaraderie like no other. The smell of popcorn, hot dogs, and hot chocolate. Simply stated, it's home, and our teams were worth watching.

One year we made it to the state basketball finals, and we had weeks of pep rallies, decorating cars for the cavalcade to Columbus, staying together in hotels, and adorning our bodies with all things red and blue. We had with each other the time of our lives. Those boys on the court had to have felt the love of a lifetime coming from the bleachers. We were family, happy to be together, with smiles frozen on our faces. We were loud and proud, competitive and united under the umbrella of basketball. There was nowhere else we'd rather be than together as a force of nature — enthusiasm running rampant. We marched in lockstep.

Was it possible that our community was so tight that aberrations were threatening? Or was it possible that backlash might trump compassion if one of us stepped too far out of line? I think back to that time in history when unmarried pregnant girls were not allowed in class, but their boyfriends were, when interracial dating was absolutely verboten, when divorce still carried a stigma, particularly if you were the female. Loving hands around each member of the Church were a strong support providing one didn't rattle the cage too much. Too much, and the scaffolding might begin to waver.

I believe our glass houses were built simultaneously with the duality of love and fear. Structures strong and conflicting, towering and fragile. The spires on a cathedral of contradictions. I mean, a bracelet with "WWJD?" just left me bewildered at times. If you're unfamiliar with the WWJD movement, let me explain. It's simple really. In the early 90s there were these bracelets with "WWJD" on them. The "WWJD" stood for "What Would Jesus Do?" It was an attempt at making us think about how Jesus might have responded to a given situation before we made our own choice of a response. It was an attempt to be more like him. We were taught to love others, give unselfishly, and show kindness to all, particularly the less fortunate. This foundation of compassion and aid was and is, in my mind, the glory of the Catholic Church.

The reverse side was the fear of judgment instilled if one fell short of the goal. Fall *really* short, and the fires of Hell awaited you. Fall *moderately* short, and your sentence was reduced to a yet-to-be-determined stint in Purgatory. I was never able to reconcile this with an "all-Loving God" who promoted forgiveness of others. If He wanted me to forgive others, wouldn't it make sense that He would model that same behavior? I mean, if we're going to anthropomorphize God, then let's be consistent. I decided to begin arguing that point early on as I learned the strategy of confession. This was another ongoing conversation with my mother who never floundered in her conviction and my "being on the other side" lasted a lifetime. Hell, Purgatory, and the Final Judgment produced indecipherable static in my mind. Add Limbo to the mix, and my receiver just clicked off.

I'm going to assume that the concept of Hell is a familiar one. Depending on the religious belief, a person may land in Hell for committing a mortal sin (worse than a venial sin) and not confessing it before death. Or another may pass through the fiery gates if she hasn't yet accepted Jesus as her Lord and Savior. The dogma differs according to religious persuasion. From Hell, there is no escape.

Purgatory, on the other hand, has an escape clause. After death, I could be sent to Purgatory to do time. The length of my sentence depends on my transgressions and on the quantity of prayers, indulgences, and repentance I have done, or someone has done in my name. At least, this is how I heard it. I'm pretty sure this is also how most of us heard it at the time. So, if I were to be sent to Purgatory, it would be only a matter of time before the gates of Heaven would open for me. I just had to tough it out 'til then.

Limbo, the holding cell for any soul not baptized before death, was officially retracted in 2007 by the Catholic Church. According to the 800-year-old teaching, Limbo was the destination for unbaptized babies. The first MaryBob (my parents had a stillborn girl with my same name before I was born) is in Limbo because she never had the chance to be baptized. Is she to stay there forever? Who made up that rule? This particular belief haunted my mother throughout her life, and it angered me that someone had told her this. I was angered because my mom would get tears in her eyes whenever anyone made a reference to MaryBob, the stillborn, not-baptized-before-gone baby. Occasionally, my mother would wonder out loud about what she might do to get her out of Limbo and into Heaven. Or better yet, what she could have done before the birth to guarantee the baby's survival. Why would anyone *ever* invent such a horror story and then promote it in the name of "God's love"? Something was terribly wrong in my mind.

So, what would Jesus do? I was pretty sure from what I had learned of Jesus, he would have gone another route entirely in dealing with personal transgressions. I felt that even the worst offenders had to have previously experienced something dreadful to end up doing whatever it was they did. Whatever that thing was it lead them to the awful choices they made. Jesus would love them, even in their "horribleness." My mother used to say, "It's the ones you're least inclined to love who need your love the most." That sounded more like Jesus to me than the idea of condemning anyone to the fires of Hell.

What I began to consciously struggle with were teachings I believed to be exclusionary. Love everyone, but beware of those who push the framework. Holy Communion, you know, the body and blood of Christ? My lack of understanding or acceptance did not devalue the privilege, yet a priest's decision to deny it to a divorcée, a non-Catholic, a person "not in a state of grace" perplexed me beyond measure. Those denials felt like stones of judgment no matter how I sliced it. Love, but only under pre-described conditions. Not the unconditional love espoused by Jesus.

In elementary school my classmates and I all brought our breakfast to school on the mornings we went to Mass. Since we had to fast for three hours before receiving Holy Communion, and Mass was said at 8:30, there was no chance to eat before school. My mom's fried egg sandwiches with mustard were a hit. I occasionally brought two in case someone else wanted one. Sometimes, when one of us forgot and accidentally ate before school, we had to stay seated in the pew while everyone else went up to communion. I always felt sorry for whoever that was, especially if it was me. It felt mean to make one of us stay back when the rest filed up to the communion railing just because we had eaten breakfast. Our teachers made such a big deal out of our having the privilege of experiencing the body and blood of Christ that being denied it was maddening at best. Who made up that edict anyway? Pretty sure it wasn't Jesus. And add to that my friend's dad and mom who weren't permitted to go to communion because he had been divorced, and she wasn't a Catholic. Once again, I'm thinking that wasn't a Jesus call.

I heard what I perceived to be mixed messages for years that disquieted me, and any explanations only fueled my fire of distrust. For me the answers were not in the faith I had been given as a child. You might ask, "Why not try the Bible, MaryBob?" Well, I did, and all I could hear were the interpretations I had been taught. I tried praying more, going to Mass with more intention, giving myself lectures, asking my mother for guidance, reciting the rosary more, everything I knew to talk myself out of my growing unease. What are we to do with the fear of disappointing or infuriating the Church, our families or friends? Fear of making a move when we know our souls are crying for change. Fear of going to hell after we die and fear of lying on our death bed wondering what might have been, if only we had had the courage to step out. So, what does one do? Take the risks and pray that everything will be ok, or stay put in the name of peace, all the while dying a quiet death that is socially acceptable?

On the canvas of my life are painted the faces of my beloved family and friends. I hold them dear like buried treasure. A young coworker once said to me, "It seems to me that everyone you care about has their own compartment in your heart." She was right. And there is no limit to the number of rooms there. I learned in my early 20s that my insatiable desire to experience the unfamiliar might send mixed signals to those whom I cherished most. I could unwittingly confound them in the living of my own life.

Remember that during our trip to Guatemala I decided to learn Spanish? I held that intention so fiercely there was not a snowball's chance in hell that I was going to be denied the opportunity. That baby was going to be born. All I had to do was figure out the how. Let the planning begin! In my excitement, I now wonder if I inadvertently sent out a signal of, "I'll catch you later, on my way back through" to my family and friends. If so, it was never my intention. I just knew I had to go and get this thing done.

Something Ventured, Something Lost

My parents and I had chosen the Technological Institute in Monterrey, Mexico after a couple of false starts. From my university student body of approximately 3,400 students I was one of *two* who had their minds set on studying abroad. It was not such a popular thing to do in those days. My other adventurer had decided on Ireland for her sojourn. Wanting to study where I didn't know the language left some of my friends scratching their heads. I'll bet they thought I had lost my marbles, and those marbles were loose rolling down the street. The student body I was set to adopt had thirteen thousand, and only *eleven* of us were English-speaking.

I landed in Monterrey, and I cried for weeks until I was finally able to understand at least some of what was being said around me. My roommate spoke no English. I had determined that if I was to learn Spanish I had to spend more time with my Mexican classmates and little to no time with my fellow English-speakers. After about week six I realized I understood most of what people were saying. My frustration leveled off, and the learning and adventuring began. I had the time of my life and fell in love with all things Mexican.

The markets were vibrant, the city loud, and as hard as I tried I couldn't get myself lost on the city buses. Jumping on any city bus that pulled into campus, I would ride it until I felt like getting off, wander around that part of town for an hour or so, and get back on another bus there until I finally found my way back to campus. I did it alone to force myself to speak Spanish. It was, after all, 1974. A different time and place. My friends and I rode horses in the mountains, climbed onto the roof of the university library to watch the stars, ate doughnuts across the street late at night, and practiced all the bad words I could learn in one sitting. I clawed my way through French class in Mexico. A foreign language being taught in a different foreign language. I learned to "bargain" in the market and with taxi drivers. This particular skill was not one my mother appreciated when my parents visited. She felt sorry for the vendors I was haggling with. I remember haggling with a taxi driver who was transporting me and a group of Japanese students. They couldn't speak English. I couldn't speak Japanese, and none of us were very good at Spanish. *It was a moment.*

One night our dorm was awakened by loud music. A girl down the hall was being serenaded by a mariachi band paid for by an admirer. They were out on the sidewalk, outside her window, and since our dorms had no glass in the windows, we all decided to join in. It felt like heaven on earth to me.

Little was I aware the glass house I had left on my home campus was getting its windows fogged up. The friends with whom I had spent the last two years of my life somehow interpreted my semester away as "I don't care about you anymore." They decided to all get a house off campus... without me. They gave me the news one day when I called them from Mexico. I recall their words, hanging up the phone and sitting down inside the public phone booth in tears. How could they do that? Did they forget I was coming back or did they just not care anymore? Outta sight outta mind? I was devastated. Did they reject me because they felt I had rejected them? I didn't have the emotional wherewithal to develop that idea at the time, but I think there must have been some truth in it. I had made a decision to go long before I met them. Had I made a mistake in leaving? Who was I going to be with when I got back home? Would they even be around anymore? Why didn't they ask me about it before they decided? Maybe you're just not as smart as you think, MaryBob. Maybe they're the ones who have it all together. You just messed up the works with your big ideas. You deserve this. After all, you're the one who left, not them. At that moment I withdrew into myself, and those friendships would never be the same. I believe it was the first time in my life that my insatiable curiosity cost me dearly. It would not be the last. I had rattled the scaffolding too much. There was nothing to be done. Their decision had been made, and it was clear I was not the same person who had left five months earlier.

Living another way of life has a profound effect on any psyche. The obvious change, upon my return, was my speaking a different language. What wasn't so obvious was my new outlook on life, and it had nowhere to express itself. My experiences in Mexico caused me to understand the joy of that culture, and the importance of celebration. What I had found entertaining before going was no longer entertaining. Back on my home campus it was the same old same old. I was combatting a serious case of reverse culture shock and didn't know it. I had not known such a thing existed before living it, and I wish I had understood more. Being only one of two students on campus who chose to "exchange" explains why there was little attention paid to the emotional impact of going away, staying away, and returning to one's home culture. When I arrived in Mexico I didn't fit in, until I finally did. When I came home I didn't fit it, and since the old me was gone, I felt adrift. I recognized my friends were only politely interested in my previous endeavors, nor was I interested in theirs. It wasn't anyone's fault. My mother was right. She used to say, "You can't recreate what used to be. It will not be the same."

I had set out to achieve a goal, had crossed the finish line, and found myself running the victory lap alone. Even then, would I have changed any of it? Absolutely not! I knew I had lost some of what was dear to me, but I also knew I had gained a belief in myself that no one could take away. The seeker in me was just getting warmed up. I was simultaneously proud of myself and wondering what the hell had gone wrong. I wanted to fit in and stand apart at the same time. I had chosen a different route, and the trail was only beginning to get bumpy.

Before I get too far down this road, let me make something clear, *and I mean clear.* My response to what I was being shown was *my* response. I am not blaming anybody or anything. I made choices, and the results gave me ample opportunity to decide who I wanted to be in this world.

Learn by Example

My loving parents were devoted to the Catholic Church, and my dad was one of the co-founders of the St. Vincent de Paul society in town. The other was his friend Joe, who owned the neighborhood grocery. Together they shared the responsibility of feeding those in need. Joe was one of my dad's best friends, and the two of them were a force of nature when it came to helping the less fortunate. I don't know how he and dad came to their decision, but Joe lives in so many of my memories. Our families knew each other since day one, and his son and I were in the same class at school. His market was where we sent people who called or knocked on our door asking for help. He and dad fished together, bowled together, and played horse shoes together. Since his grocery was just down the street from our house, I loved making excuses to go there once I got my driver's license. I also remember that he let me call him "Joe" when I was a little girl. That was the best thing ever! These men were two powerful examples of the Church at its best.

I mentioned earlier that in our house, we had two telephones. One for personal use and the other for funeral home business and calls from "Saint V's." The callers asking for food or shelter were a high priority for my parents. I can't count the number of times I heard my dad say to the person on the other end of the line, "Go to O'Brien's market and get what you need. Just tell Joe it's for Saint Vincent's."

My parents sold tickets, bought candy, sponsored sports teams, attended every ice cream social and spaghetti supper known to man. They clothed families and rented trucks at

Christmas to deliver baskets of food and toys. My parents simply loved people, and looking up at them I never wanted to see disappointment in their eyes. Their goodness was palpable to me. It seemed to me the pull to do more was a constant tug for them.

Their example was not lost on any of us, and my all-time favorite memory is of one particular winter evening. It was already dark outside, and we had just finished cleaning up the dinner dishes. I glanced out the window overlooking the parking lot and saw a dilapidated white station wagon with a gigantic, and I mean gigantic, white crucifix tied with rope to the top. This wagon had pulled into our parking lot and was just sitting there, so my dad went out to see what they wanted. It wasn't long before he came in the back door followed by a family of ten, two parents and eight kids. They had been driving to I-don't-know-where and had run out of money and food.

Somehow, they had found their way to our house, so my mom welcomed them in, opened the refrigerator and pulled out every chicken leg, cheese wedge and loaf of bread available to feed that family. While we prepared the food the eight kids tore through our house, up and down the stairs, in and out of the doors, jumped on the beds, until finally their parents corralled them at our dining room table. They ate, and as they left that evening my dad gave them money for gas and directed them to a place to stay for the night.

The minute the door closed my self-righteous self and I started in about how disrespectful the kids had been. About how they had shouted and grabbed everything they saw, and how the parents had no control. They had left fingerprints on the walls and jumped up and down on our beds. I went on for about one minute. I was silenced by my dad saying, "You don't know what it's like to walk in someone else's shoes, so hush." Bam! There it was again. He had made that statement time and again, only on this occasion he looked me in the eye. We stood for more than a second or two, eyes locked. He had not raised his voice, but he was not kidding. I had better get the message and fast. Another game-changing moment for me. The power of his belief in that single concept poured into me like new concrete on a driveway, made to form, still drying, but set to last a lifetime. "You don't know what it's like to walk in someone else's shoes." His look told me everything I'd ever need to know about someone else's behavior or attitude. It was clear. Their life experiences were not mine, so overlaying my observations of them with the filter of my own upbringing was not only ineffective, it was unkind in every way imaginable.

I'd like to say that I've held steadily to that tenet, and, no doubt, it has guided me many times. The truth is, when I was most in pain after divorcing my second husband, I was so deep in the well, my dad's voice was out of reach. At that juncture, my "blame game" was a tough match between how horrible I had been versus how horrible everyone else had been in response. It's only now that I recognize the reaction of everyone around me and including me, to that series of events. Slowly, over time, my father's words found their way back to me.

Their return began by my unconsciously citing my dad's wisdom to my children and friends. I heard myself telling them they didn't know what it was like to walk in someone else's shoes. I told them it was painful to judge others. I could see what *they* were doing, but had excluded *myself* from my own directive. I was sweeping around everyone else's doorstep, not yet seeing the potential application of this idea to the players in *my* past. My new view of life allowed me to see how we judge others when they are being judgmental. You know, like when we decide we don't like someone because they are not being nice to another someone? We do that, right? I think my dad's spirit was tapping me on the shoulder all along until one day, DING! A thought ran through my head that went something like, "Every person in that drama reacted exactly as they were supposed to according to what they believed, including you. If even one of them had done something other than what they did, you might not have had the courage to do the exploring you've done. They were walking in their shoes, and you were walking in yours. That's all that was going on. Now, what will bring you the most peace, continued self-righteousness and anger or delving into the belief that we are all doing the best we can with the skills we have in any given moment?"

Ok, I hear you, Dad. The implications and applications of that philosophy are endless in my mind. Religion, politics, race, gender, age, nationalism. Holding fast to the need to be right is a roadblock to our own expansion. How can I become the greatest expression of myself in this life, if I insist on seeing the world through my eyes only? I admit, I don't think I can.

Conflict of Conscience

I have heard it said that one's Spirit will at first whisper a suggestion to you. If unheeded, it will try again with a feather, then a stick, then a brick, until eventually, a Mack truck comes rolling down the center of your life to get your attention. At first, I could slough off any thoughts of something other than my life as it was. I taught school, mothered children, "wived" two husbands. Yep, I had my first brief marriage annulled (another theme all together) by the Church so I could marry again, should I choose. I did. My first husband was an unknown entity to my hometown friends. I believe my divorcing him was considered simply "unfortunate." Not so when I chose to divorce my second husband of sixteen years. At that point, the wrath of God came down on me like a mountain rock slide.

I had really done it this time! All acceptance I had enjoyed during my life was blasted by a tornado of disapproval. In one fell swoop I became a pariah to those who had laughed with me only days before my decision became public fodder. My family included. At the time, I couldn't see their point. Again. Why would a decision for my life cause them to react so fiercely? My glass house came crashing down around me. What happened to the glass houses of my friends and family I'm not able to say.

On another note, let's look at my concept of marriage, if I even had a concept. Again, love and fear. I believe I loved, but I feared even more. I feared failure and disappointment. I had come from a long line of strong women. I mentioned earlier that my great-grandmother had been the first female bank president in the state of Ohio. Then my grandmother raised her three children after being widowed at the age of 23, my grandfather having died in the flu epidemic. My mother was the valedictorian of her class and the first female in the family to get a college degree. I was not going to be the woman in that lineup who crashed and burned. No way. I'll eat all my vegetables! You just watch!

Once I hit my teens I received strong input from my sweet mother about who was in control of the sex thing before marriage. It was the late sixties and early seventies, so the signals I received were mixed. According to my mother, and reflecting her own upbringing, the girl was the one in charge of keeping her cool. Males could not be expected to do so. Any hanky-panky, and the gauntlet fell on me. As I approached marriage, once again reflecting the then acceptable obligations as wife, she made it clear that the roles were about to be reversed. It then became the husband who rightfully determined the sex-life, once the vows were said. Excuse me? Did I hear her correctly? I was sure the signal she was sending had gotten scrambled somehow, and I was not prepared for that! I remember exactly where I was standing in the house, when she made that morsel clear to me. Surely, she was not serious.

She told me that once married it would be my duty to be available to my husband. If she were alive today, she may say I heard that wrong, and maybe I did, but I took it to heart. I was stunned and angry, my defiance surging forward as my respect for her held me back. What I heard was, "Once you're married, your life is no longer yours." Slam the prison doors shut! The term "wedlock" took on a whole new meaning in that instant. Emphasis on the second syllable.

My mother's love for me was fierce, and I knew that. Her word held sway over many choices I had made for most of my life. My parents had a loving, mutually respectful relationship, and now she throws this out? The inconsistency in her directive left me speechless. Although my Catholic education was mostly conservative, the impact of the feminist movement was not lost on me. Was I expected to pretend I had never heard the words of Gloria Steinem or Bella Abzug? Was the seeker and adventurer in me destined to remain locked up in the prison cell of wifedom in honor of what had always been? Whoa, Nelly! That's what I call trying to ride two horses to the finish line. Only one of us can succeed, and I have a feeling that victory is gonna be painful for both.

STOP THE WORLD

"I said, 'Pain and sorrow?' He (God) said, "Stay with it. The wound is the place where the Light enters you." – Rumi

My Life in the Rearview Mirror

I'm not sure as a young woman I ever had a clear picture of what my future life would look like. Some girls dream of their wedding day, the white dress, the church and eventual motherhood. Some girls dream of successful careers, breaking glass ceilings and traveling the world. Not me. I just took it as it came — assuming everything would work out fine, and there was some kind of peace in that. It was a good thing nobody ever asked me where I saw myself in five years as some interviewers do. I think my face would have gone blank with "I dunno" rolling off my tongue.

Looking in my rearview mirror, it seems 1988 was the beginning of some things, the end of others, and the beginning-of-the-end of still more. That year, my husband and I were blessed with a beautiful baby girl. We had been hoping for years, and there she was with her shiny dark eyes, looking up at us from her baby carrier. The wonder and joy of her arrival was unlike any other experience in our life. Surreal. It was love at first sight. Magical pixie dust fell from the sky onto our little family. Our son was 11 at the time, and although it wasn't love at first sight for him, we knew they would grow to care for each other, and they did.

1988: My brother and his wife decided to move out of the country, 3,000 miles from home. He had spent most of his adult life living just 2 hours away, so his departure was major. In the fall my sister — who had lived next door to my parents for over 20 years — and her new husband decided to move out of state as well. In both cases I understood why they had made their choices, and didn't blame them for taking advantage of the opportunities. For me their timing couldn't have been worse, but I wanted to be the strong one. My mother, struggling within herself on how to best care for my failing father, was sad at both departures, but would never have let either of them know. She was, after all, the matriarch. I remember saying goodbye to both of them and watching their cars drive out of the funeral home parking lot. I'm not sure what I was feeling, but "responsible" and "alone" probably topped the list. Little did I know it would be only a few weeks, and our father would be gone. I was thunderstruck by his death.

1988-At the same time my father's body succumbed to the dementia he had been battling for five years. It had first shown itself while my parents were on vacation. He had lost his keys and some cash and had accused one of the workers of stealing it from their room. My mother instantly knew something was going terribly wrong. Upon their return home she related the incident to only me, not wanting to alarm my siblings. My dad had never pointed a finger at anyone for anything in his life. Giving others the benefit of the doubt was his MO. His recent accusation was a screaming red flag. We both knew it.

As time passed he forgot more details until it became necessary for him to leave his own business for someone else to run. He knew he was no longer able to handle the particulars, but that funeral home was so much of his life. He and my mother had raised it up from birth. Not being able to tend to it tore at his heart. He would stand in the house, staring across the driveway at his lifelong work, and say to me, "I should be over there, but they won't let me." "They" being the Social Security Administration and us. We knew he could no longer care for those families in his exceptional way, and encouraging him to keep his distance was gut-wrenching.

The anger he occasionally showed was, for me, the most heartbreaking. I had yet to learn the varied manifestations of dementia, and to see him travel the emotional track from calm to sad to angry both shocked and paralyzed me. Where had my dad gone? Who was this man? Living in a town where most knew him was a blessing for our family. Before we could wrangle away his car keys, dad would drive and invariably get lost. He would forget his hat and coat somewhere, walk through the snow to his car and keep driving until he had to stop, sometimes in the next town over. The gas station manager or shop owner made the call to our house. Either they recognized him immediately, he had momentarily recalled his address and phone number, or they figured it out from his driver's license.

His presence had been such a powerful force in our family, that his decline into another world left me grasping for something to hold on to. The rock I had spent my life standing on was slipping beneath the water with no chance of retrieval. My mother, insisting she could handle it all, chose to keep him at home until it became glaringly obvious that she could not. He never had the chance to know our daughter. She arrived in the spring. In the fall my mother reluctantly admitted my father to a care facility, and a week later he left his body. The evening before he left he momentarily recognized me as I stood next to him. Sitting in a chair he reached out, wrapped his arms around my legs, and said, "I love you, honey." I wrapped my arms around his head, and replied, "I love you too, dad." That was it.

He was my forever hero, and his passing left me with one of the wheels falling off my wagon. In the beginning his illness led me to dig more deeply into my faith, but to no avail. I prayed rosary after rosary. I spoke to priest friends about the draft I felt in my chest. I lit candles, knelt in church and begged God for guidance. Nothing. I felt nothing for all my efforts. No answers. No relief. No destination calling me to move forward. My dad's laughter was gone, and no prayer or belief could ease that.

Dementia is not something to laugh at, but let me give you a little playback here to lighten it up a bit. Being born to parents who were 20 years older than those of my friends, I was forever fearful they would die when I was young. As my father fell into dementia in his later years, my mother told me I was taking it harder than my much older brother and sister. This was true, but even in his craziest moments my family was somehow able to find humor. Again, it was a gift for which I will always be grateful.

"I've got a pain in my chest," I heard him say somewhere around his 73rd birthday. Ten years earlier he had undergone bypass surgery, leaving us all watchful of his health. The snow was pouring out of the dark sky that December night. "But it only hurts when I lean back. It's ok when I lean forward."

Trying to swallow the fear and grasping for the humor my family so often employed, I replied, "Then just stay leaning forward, Dad." He chuckled. "Since you're not the ambulance driver anymore, you want me to call the hospital to have one come get you? "No," he replied, "Just let me sit out here in my chair."

My cherished mother, who had a bit of a love affair with hypochondria, decided she was having a dizzy spell, so lay down on the couch to see if it would pass, placing her arm over her eyes and breathing deeply. My dad in his recliner kept switching forward and back to see if the sharp pain continued its pattern…forward, no pain…back, stinging pain, and my mom on the couch telling me she was fine.

Lately my dad had become lethargic and forgetful, a sad turn for a man who had more friends than he could count and a smile to match his contagious laugh. I had begun mourning his passing long before his breath ever left his body. Only occasionally would my dad's spirit return now with his shiny eyes and that broad smile. This was not one of those occasions, but I decided to invoke the humor that was the family cornerstone.

Ambulances Now and Then

There I stood looking at both of them, wondering what in God's name I was going to do if I had to call two ambulances that night at the same time. This was going to be my call. I began, "Ok, I'm standing here staring at the two of you and wondering what the heck to do. This could be a scene from a dark comedy. I mean *really*. You've always been concerned about what the neighbors might think. Can you imagine what they're going to be saying tomorrow, if two ambulances roll in here and tote you two out of this house at the same time? The telephone wires are literally going to light up with everyone calling everyone else trying to figure out what went on in here tonight." That got a smile out of both of them.

This was before the implementation of 911. It would be years before our little corner of the world had that luxury.

My dad was used to driving the ambulance, not lying in the back as a passenger. Until recently dropping everything when the phone rang with an "ambulance call" was as normal to us as going to church on Sundays.

Much like a television newsman my dad was on the scene of local car accidents, suicides, and other sudden traumas. Only he did not report back to anyone. As he aged, more frequently the person requesting his services was a friend. I remember one of his friends calling for him. The friend was asking for dad to come quickly because something was terribly wrong with his wife. She died that afternoon. Later when dad walked in through the back door he was quiet. He put on his painting clothes and went outside to paint the side of the garage, never saying a word. We knew he was grieving.

Somehow, I never thought that I would ride in the back of my dad's ambulance. Then one day, in the 4th grade, my friends and I were having a contest in the cafeteria to see how long we could hold our breath. Never wanting to concede defeat, I held mine 'til I passed out, hitting my chin on the corner of the nearby metal table on my way to the floor.

Sister Gerard, the tough Irish cookie who was on duty at that moment, retrieved me from the linoleum and walked me to the office. After observing the blood pouring from my chin, she looked at me over the top of her rimless spectacles and asked, "Should we call your father's ambulance, Miss Hogenkamp?" Of course, I said, "No." That was the closest I ever came to having that experience. Thank God. The seven stitches the doctor put in my chin after school that day led my occasionally feisty mother to "clarify" some things with that nun later.

Back to the story...

Maybe an hour passed with the three of us staring at each other, and my dad eventually decided to go back to bed. My mom then felt well enough to go fry an egg. That's what she always did when she was working through some emotional event. Bacon and eggs were comfort food for mom, and I knew she was thinking about something whenever I found her standing in front of the stove with an egg ready to crack.

They had both convinced me that it was not necessary to call any ambulances. As my mom and I sat at the kitchen table reviewing the situation we heard my dad's laughter from his bedroom. He met us in the hall in his boxer shorts and t-shirt. It was one of his lucid moments. Chuckling, he opened his hand to show us what was inside. Therein lay a 9-volt battery and a quarter. We didn't get it. My mom and I looked at each other, then at him, questioning.

"It's no wonder my chest stung when I leaned back. These were both in my shirt pocket," he explained. We still didn't get it. "Every time I leaned back they touched each other and created an arc."

"An arc? What?! You mean an electrical arc?! Are you kidding? You mean that pain was coming from that damned battery? And we thought it might be a heart attack? Where'd you get that battery, Dad?"

"I don't know. It must have been lying around somewhere, but that explains the chest pain," he said with a smile. The relief burst from my throat and we three laughed 'til we cried.

"You can't make this stuff up!" I heard myself crying to my mom.

As my father's dementia deepened over the next few months I would recall this moment at those times when I missed him the most. Remembering it now, so many years later, still makes me smile. I suspect he's smiling too.

Several years after my father's death my mother allowed herself to be convinced to sell their funeral home to a large international company. It was a sad day. I remember her saying to me the morning she was to sign the documents, "I wish I had never gotten myself into this." I told her she didn't have to sign the papers, but she felt it was too late. Several years later that same company declared bankruptcy, leaving my mother with nothing. After 50 years of dreaming and dedication, my parent's hard work went up in a puff of smoke. Gone with nothing to show for it.

The Collapse of Pleasantville

Around that same time our son seemed to slide further and further away from what we had envisioned his life to be as a young man. He became disobedient, surly. We tried everything we knew, but there was no getting him to conform. The initial disappointment eventually led to frustration and anger. We tried everything from encouragement to bribery, punishment, and counseling. Still his grades fell along with his willingness to cooperate. He seemed angry at someone or something, and so were we at him and at each other.

Both my husband and I had been raised in the same small community, and both families ran local businesses. Being concerned about what the neighbors might think was deeply ingrained in our psyches. I was, after all, a teacher, and my own son was failing his classes in the same high school where we had both attended and taught. As his reputation for finding trouble grew I became embarrassed. Again, what would everyone think of me? Of our family? This worry about the opinion of others was not a new thing. Friends offered suggestions, guidance, and criticisms. The criticisms landed on fertile soil in my mind. I was already questioning my own parenting skills. My husband and I had different ideas on how to approach the situation, and the rift between the three of us began to grow long and wide. Our son's school work remained unfinished, and his tremendous talent in sports began falling to waste. He was eventually declared ineligible to participate in baseball and wrestling, leaving him more free time to find trouble.

As he grew into his teens the concerns became more serious. What started as failures in school slid into scrapes with the local police. There were times we didn't know where he was, who he was with, or what he might be doing. I continued to believe we could rescue him if we could just love him enough, spend hours talking it out, working through the tribulations. I held fast to the concept that our son had a good heart, and would someday correct his own path, which he eventually did. Others thought punishment was the answer.

As sorrowful as that time was for us, we do find humor now in some of his antics. I mean, how many kids teach themselves to drive *in the 7th grade?* Except for kids who grow up in rural communities, not many. We did not live on a farm, yet our son took it upon himself to get behind the wheel at twelve years of age. He and one of his friends thought it a good idea to take our two cars out cruising one evening when we had gone to the movies with another couple. Only mistake? They drove in front of a friend's house who happened to be looking out her window at the time. Oops!

We returned home unsuspecting, both cars sitting where we had left them. Moments later the phone rang, and my friend started asking questions. Well, after the inquisition, the proverbial shit hit the fan, and off we went on yet one more trip to "discipline paradise." It was not pretty.

We can laugh about it now, and today I thank my son for what he taught me. He taught me that we all have our own path. He taught me that we are all doing the best we can with the skills we have. The opinions of others are just that, *opinions*. They do not determine who we are in this world, nor can they quantify our worth or contribution to society. His actions forced me to look inside myself for answers, and for that I am eternally grateful. It wasn't apparent for many years, but I see now that my response to his behavior was the impetus for my own growth. He is a blessing to me in more ways than I can name here. Today we can laugh and appreciate some of what went on then.

Today we are friends both making our way through this life the best we know how. My son and I speak openly of those years, and recognize the part each of us played in the drama. It was not something I would wish on anyone, and still we're proud of ourselves for holding tightly to our relationship. He calls and asks my input on any variety of subjects, and we have learned to find humor in each other again. It took time, intention, and trust. We chose to each live our truth and let love guide us. That one choice has proven invaluable.

Prior to my decision to divorce, what wasn't so funny was the growing animosity between my husband and our son, and my deepening unease with the entire situation. The shoes I was wearing were not those of my husband, and we saw the world differently. Neither of us were wrong, and neither of us were right. We were just standing at opposite ends of the discipline spectrum, and could not make our way to the middle. He thought I was too forgiving, and I thought he was too heavy-handed. We had been raised under different circumstances, and either approach might have been effective if we hadn't spent most of our time arguing about which one to apply. My playing "good cop" and his insisting on what I considered to be harsh discipline resulted in the formation of a bottomless chasm between my son and his father. I probably could have played my cards differently, but I don't think I would have. I clung to the idea of my son's inherent goodness.

I never knew where it started between them. Was it because he was my son from my first marriage? Was it because my husband and I had differing ideas on what was effective correction? Or was it simply life happening as we went along? Regardless, the hateful feelings between them intensified. What we earlier considered to be frustrating yet harmless pranks escalated to being potentially dangerous, and our house grew thick with a silent resentment others couldn't see. Not only between my son and his father, but between his father and me. We had spent years trying to find a solution. There was none. I felt helpless and out of options. Our son was not going to graduate from high school with his classmates. What next?

By that time, my husband and I were at odds about almost everything. Our differing approaches had spilled over into other areas of our life. We kept up a good front, and even maybe thought to ourselves that things were going to be ok, but in the end, they just weren't. It felt to me like we were growing in different directions.

I had expectations that marriage would fill in the gaps where loneliness was holed up. This wasn't a conscious awareness at the time, but I can see it now. He and I were great together when we were in a social circle. We had the most wonderful experiences with our families and friends! We bicycled thousands of miles with a pack of friends over several summers. We vacationed at the beach with family. We both had good jobs, yet at home the tension grew. It was inside our home that I felt most alone.

Unconsciously, I tried to fill that hole with everything I could think of — leading student groups to Latin America and Europe, roller blading, taking Jazzercise classes with my sister, inviting students to our house to cook, going to grad school, learning to be an AP teacher. In retrospect I kept myself busy, not only because I loved all of the activities I had chosen, but also because I didn't know how to save my relationship with my husband. What I wanted more than anything was for both of us to be able to say what we were thinking without the other going into defense mode. Our relationship had contracted into a choice between superficialities or vitriol. My desire to keep talking about all of it was about as effective as his desire to not talk at all. Eventually, I convinced him to go with me to speak to a counselor. I, apparently, was the one with the concern, so it became my problem to solve. That was his only visit. In my mind we were simply, profoundly, irrevocably mismatched. It wasn't anyone's fault. We just were.

My husband was a good man from a good family, and our families were friends. We were both raised under the Catholic umbrella, so our values were similar. Our communities intersected on a regular basis. We had similar interests, and enjoyed each other's company at social events. My husband had initially been in business with his father. We later decided it would be a good idea for him to go into business with my brother's company running my father's former funeral home. That decision tightened the bond between them, and they became even closer friends.

My family *adored* this man. He had been a part of us for sixteen years, and only my mother knew of my growing angst. In my eyes ours was no longer a marriage. It was a dead zone. The days were filled with anger or silence except when we put on our social faces for the general public. I sought the help of a psychologist, hoping maybe he could talk me out of what I was thinking. As time passed he became one of the few people in which I could confide my feelings. My world was crumbling in front of my eyes. My father and his business were things of the past. My son was ruining his life. I was walking through my marriage as an actor on a stage. All of my praying and pleading with God was fruitless. I had nowhere to go with my roiling discomfort.

The Inner Battle

Have you ever been in the battle of your life, and the one you are fighting is *you*? There were two parts of me having it out with each other. "I gotta get outta here." "You have everything." "Sit down and hush." "I can't live like this." "Like what? You got it all." What started out as a harmless cat fight eventually turned into a match to the death. Every waking hour, and even in my sleep, the match played out. This was serious, and one of these players was going down.

Me #1:

Is this it? Am I expected to replay this same scene over and over again until I die? Wake up every morning wondering what could go sideways today? What piece of shit is going to hit the fan before we go to sleep tonight? Am I to forever pretend that everything is alright, when it sure as hell is not? Put on my veneer and make sure the glue job is tight? Our house is less than happy once the door is closed. There is never going to be peace here. It's all gone to shit. Is this how love feels? I've tried everything I know to make this work, and it's still not working. There must be more to life than this. We've spent so much of our time in drama, we don't even know each other anymore. I don't think we even like each other anymore. I'd rather be alone than be here in this tension. I'm so damned lonely, and I live in a house with people in it. I can't do this. Stop the world, I want to get off!

Me #2:

What the hell is the matter with you? Stop talking nonsense. Are you nuts? You have it all. The good husband, the
beautiful home, the two children, the great job, the loving
families and friends on both sides, and even the minivan!
Your family loves your husband, and you love his family. He
works with your brother, and both families have owned well-
known businesses and been active members of the Catholic
Church in this town for decades. There is no getting out of
this, and you know it. This is a knot that cannot be untied,
girl. You're being selfish. You're being stupid. You're just
plain crazy. You want a second divorce? How you gonna
explain *that*? Most people would give anything for what you
have. Sit down and just shut up! It's not that bad.

Me #1:

And the Church! I've had enough of its million rules, regu-
lations, and sins. It's all bullshit. There is nothing there for
me. How can any priest tell me what to do or not do? Who
the hell died and left them in charge anyway? Obey the
Church and its commandments?

Everyone thinks there is a perfectly happy couple living
in this beautiful house. They haven't heard the raised voices
or the deafening silence when something goes wrong. I feel
like I'm suffocating. I fake it every day hoping it will get better, but it doesn't

Me #2:

Oh, everyone has conflict. Get over it. Lonely? What are you
talking about? You spend all day every day with dozens of different people including your family. How can you possibly
be lonely? It will pass. You think your little hissy-fit is going
to change all of that? Maybe this is just a mid-life crisis. You

think you feel guilty now for thinking all this stuff? Imagine how guilty you're going to feel if you act on these thoughts? That's the kind of guilt that might kill a person. You'll break your mother's heart and your husband's heart. It's a good thing your dad is not here to see this. He's probably rolling over in his grave right now. Maybe you should be in your grave instead of him.

I told you earlier I did not have a five-year plan for my life, but I was pretty sure this was *not* what I had in mind. And some members of that close community of ours felt it their duty to tell us how we could have handled things differently with our son and our marriage. *Really?* They simply didn't know what they didn't know. All the love and religion in the world couldn't restore the gilded steeples of my psyche. There was nothing that could catch the gold falling from the life I had built.

There simply had to be another way! I searched my soul for longer than anyone knew for an answer to my angst and found nothing. I felt I had washed out to sea without any chance of return, hoping I might drown. Any possible solution looked like emotional and social suicide. Which casket would I choose if my parent's funeral home still existed? I would never be able to explain myself so my family and friends might understand. Of that I was certain. My husband and I could not have looked more like Barbie and Ken if we had been made by Mattel. I make that joke, but it felt too true. I'm pretty sure from the outside looking in, that things looked rather perfect.

As time passed my despair deepened. I hadn't allowed anyone into my world. I was on auto-pilot, and my body was beginning to feel the effects. Although I had discussed my growing unease with my husband on more than one occasion, I believe he thought it would pass eventually. It didn't.

The web of our family and social connections was so tightly woven, my stepping away would, without a doubt, unravel the silk and send it crashing to the floor. That is exactly what happened.

In retrospect, I realize now that my inevitable choice resulted from my spirit telling me that if I was to survive, I had better make a move. I was beyond being lonely for someone else. I was lonely for me. If someone had said that to me at the time, I'm not sure I could have heard them. I just didn't know who I was anymore, and I didn't know where to look to find me. A source greater than any I had previously known held me when I couldn't hold myself. The response from family and friends, upon hearing of my decision to divorce my husband, was swift and furious. Only two people ever asked me why I had made the decision to leave, and at the time I couldn't put it into words. Knowing what I know now, it's not difficult to see why the judgments flew like rocks as I exited that glass cathedral. Once again love and fear were hand in hand. The same family and friends who had lovingly hugged me the day before suddenly spewed righteousness and anger. I was shut out. I didn't exist. It was as if I were never born. The cold was bitter.

I had expected people would be shocked and saddened. I hadn't expected to be ostracized. Totally and completely. For life. My sister, her husband, one life-long friend and several friends from work the only ones willing to even look me in the eye. For a full six months my mother, who had been my life-long best friend, would not speak to me. Swallowed in guilt, I withdrew. In my mind, I had destroyed any years she had left in this life. Once again, to say I had disappointed her would be an understatement. Only this time it was life-threatening to both of us. Stepping now into her shoes I feel her utter disbelief and confusion, but at the time I was her daughter. I was flabbergasted, astonished, muted by her treatment of me. My disbelief and hurt were volcanic, boiling lava rolling just under the crust of my everyday appearance. I thought blood ran thicker than water. Apparently not. That curve ball was thrown with deadly force.

Eventually, she and I would be able to carry on a stilted conversation, but it was never the same. She passed away three and half years later, still befuddled by my choices. I would have been too, I suppose. My brother who could make me laugh til I cried, and whom I had adored for forty-two years turned away along with the rest of my family and friends. If, at the time, I could have chosen to possess a super power, it would have been to be invisible. As it turned out I didn't have to choose. I was.

After reeling from the intensity of their fury I continued to awaken each morning hoping that on that day one of them would call me to say hi — that they would want to return to the family harmony that was the hallmark of my childhood and young adulthood. That they would apologize for cutting my limb from the family tree. I still clung to the hope they would adhere to the one of the primary tenets of Jesus's teachings – forgiveness! But the phone never rang. My family was gone. Their decision was final.

Disconnected

No, let me correct that previous statement. I did receive one call. It was made to inform me that I was *not* being invited to the celebration of my sister-in-law becoming a U.S. citizen. "We had to make a choice, and we've all decided it would be better for your ex-husband to be there instead of you."

How does one respond to that, coming from the family with whom I had spent every holiday, birthday and vacation for my whole life? At first, I didn't say anything. I remember lying on the floor of my living room as I was listening to the words being spoken, tears rolling back into my ears.

"OK." I hung up. I couldn't move. Was this real? How long could my family continue this freeze out? Did they really think this was a good idea? If my dad were here, he would not stand for this. Dad! Please! I need you! At that point, I believe it had been over a year since making my decision to leave. Elisabeth Kübler Ross once identified the five stages of grief as denial, anger, bargaining, depression and acceptance. She made clear they were not necessarily to be experienced in a linear fashion, but might manifest themselves concurrently or out of order. During that time denial and anger were raging in me. How could people who had previously declared such love exhibit such viciousness? I then recognized I was on an island staring across an endless sea. Alone. This was my new life, and I had better figure out what the hell I was going to do with it. My guilt for having caused it all was epic.

I lay in my single bed at night trying to figure out why I was so damned needy, why I had felt alone for so many years. I wanted to undo all of it and not undo any of it simultaneously. I wanted to talk to my family and feel that they could hear what I was saying, but I was so ridden with guilt and blame I couldn't even think of asking them to listen. At the same time, I knew they wouldn't understand, so why even try.

Beginning then, I could no longer "walk in someone else's shoes." Mine were the only shoes I could walk in, and I had no idea in which direction to step. There was fire at every turn. Even the grocery store was not safe. I recall turning down an isle in our local grocery and seeing an old friend at the other end. We made eye contact, and without hesitation she turned her cart around to avoid meeting me.

There I stood staring at her back. *Did she really just do that?* Am I that evil? I picked my purse out of the cart, leaving it in the aisle and fled to my car, unable to hold my tears. Simply incredulous. Eventually, I would allow myself to see through her eyes, but not at that moment. I didn't need to step into another fire. My own fury enveloped me. How could they?

Curtain drops and up to the microphone step two men; Deepak Chopra and Eknath Easwaran.

What Doesn't Kill You

"Hard times arouse an instinctive desire for authenticity." – Coco Chanel

Seeking Spiritual Solace

So how did I get from the confessional to Deepak Chopra? How or where I found him is beyond me, but thank heavens I did. You believe in angels? Spirit Guides? Messengers? He was one for me. Almost a year before I left my marriage his book *The Seven Spiritual Laws of Success* had found its way into my hands, in cassette form. After all, it was 1996. I had become more than desperate for relief from my own thinking. Imploring the God of my childhood left me exhausted and hopeless, and talking to anyone — family, friends, priests, was not an option. I knew what their solutions would be. "Be grateful for what you have and endure. God never gives you more than you can handle." I had already been given more than I could handle, and it wasn't going well. The grit of my Midwestern upbringing was falling to pieces.

For the first time in my life I was looking ahead, and all I could see was more distance and silence. The moments of joy were few and far between. I felt backed into a corner I could not escape. Deepak's voice on a strip of magnetic tape was my lifeline. I recall sitting in the car in the garage not wanting to turn off the engine as I listened to his calm voice tell of our energy fields of pure potentiality. I heard him explain that our consciousness is one of all possibilities and unlimited creativity. We are limited by our own thinking, and if we can see our world differently we can change it. I did not really understand intellectually what he was saying but my soul knew it was what I needed. The idea of there being more to understand, more to explore, more to life than what we thought we knew was oxygen to my soul. And science was beginning to have a relationship with spirituality? Deepak discussed reincarnation, using his grandmother's explanation of a worn-out car as an analogy. He explained how he spent his days in Catholic school and after school his grandmother and he spent time together. To help him understand the concept she used an old car that just didn't run well anymore. As I heard it she told him the time would come for her to put her body down in favor of her next incarnation. She wouldn't really leave him. She would just get a newer model to run around in. Whether that's how he meant it or not, that's how I heard it, and the concept rang true for me in that moment. It was such a relief to know that this experience would not be my only experience.

One rather large problem, in my world reincarnation was a concept we referenced only in ridicule. "Be careful with that New Age material," my mother warned. "The Church sees it as evil." Although my mother was educated, independent, and worked outside the home, disagreeing with Church teachings was not in her repertoire. Nope. Not happening. No need to spend time wondering about that reincarnation thing. The Church says it ain't so, so it ain't so. My mother is cringing now at my usage of the word "ain't."

Before I moved out, and as I was thinking the unthinkable, I continued to teach high school, and those hours in the classroom with my students were my lifeblood. Their energy, curiosity, and general love of life kept me sane. I will be forever indebted to them, and they didn't even know of the medicine they were dispensing. My personal world lay in ruin, so going to work was my reprieve from all that. Standing in front of 25 different kids every hour or so does not offer the option of being distracted. I was forced to focus on the task at hand. I now recall saying to myself on some days just before the bell rang for class, "Shows on! Bring up the curtain!" As that curtain lifted, so did my spirit. Thank God I had no choice but to be "on." In the midst of it all we laughed our way through scuba diving lessons and went to Mexico for credit in PE and Spanish. It was shortly after this adventure that my body began to show signs of my emotional upheaval.

I was forty-two years old, in the prime of life. After returning from Mexico I went for a routine checkup at my OB/GYN's office. This doctor had been a friend of ours for years. His kids were my students in school, and our families knew each other. My visit was going as always until he started asking me unusual questions.

"Do you feel ok? Have you been under unusual stress? When's the last time you saw your family doctor? Finally, he gave me instructions to get a prescription filled, go home immediately, take three days off work, and don't move until I could see my GP. Why? My blood pressure was 195/130, or some crazy number like that. What?! I just came back from being ninety feet under water in the Gulf of Mexico not knowing I was dangerously hypertensive. What was going on?

I knew. Immediately. My anger, uncertainty, and frustration were eating me alive. Literally. Little did I know then how our bodies communicate with us, giving us insight into our own journey through this life. I began the regimen of medicine needed to control my blood pressure, and at the same time delved into other avenues of controlling my hypertension on my own. No way was I going to be taking medicine for the rest of my life! I felt old and crumbling, totally freaked out. There had to be an answer somewhere besides in a bottle of pills.

I had always been active, so it wasn't a question of adding exercise. I stopped eating salt, and if you know me, you know that was a challenge. You can have your cupcakes, just give me a bag of chips! Remember, this was before the internet was so accessible, so I was holed up in the library at school flipping through periodicals. I searched everywhere I knew for alternative approaches to healing myself, even though I knew convention said it was going to be medicine. I was terrified of living and at the same time petrified I might die. Either the guilt I was feeling for the disappointment I was about to cause everyone would kill me or my failing health would.

What jumped out at me was meditation. Meditation was a word I had heard used repeatedly by Deepak Chopra and Eknath Easwaran, and here it was again. The word even sounded "otherworldly" to me. I placed an order for meditation cassettes and hoped they would arrive wrapped in plain brown paper, so the mailman and neighbors wouldn't know what was inside. The first time I hit "play" on my cassette player, I considered the possibility that I was about to take leave of my senses. The words and sounds emanating from that machine were more foreign than any language I had ever studied. Nobody I knew was doing this, and I was sure I wasn't ever going to be telling anyone about it. Wrong again.

Every day I set my alarm for 4:30 a.m. to give myself thirty minutes each morning to meditate before arriving at school at 7:00. Thus, began my odyssey into a realm of belief I never knew and never anticipated. A thin ray of light squeezing through a hairline fracture in my understanding of this universe. For the first few weeks it took everything I had not to throw in the towel on this new idea. My mind was on overload, and it felt like a runaway train. I squirmed and rocked in that chair. I began, quit, and then began again I don't know how many times. I decided to calm myself, and I was not giving up, even though I really wanted to. I got a drink of water. I made coffee. I talked to myself. I went to the bathroom. Weeks passed before I could sit, breathe, and listen to what my spirit had to say to me. I was in scary, uncharted territory, and I didn't much like it at first. What I wanted was to take a trip somewhere. Anywhere. Create a school project, make lesson plans. Do anything but sit and look at myself.

I pasted myself into my chair and ultimately allowed my meditation to sink in, giving me the strength to clear the path to greater experiences than I had ever known. I took it one step at a time, some days bushwhacking, some days weed-eating and others resting in the sun or rain. It was never the same two days in a row. I got comfortable with slipping and falling, and I was still a beginner, but the brief, sweet feeling of peace kept urging me on.

Several months later, celebrating New Year's Eve at the beach with my family, I found myself sitting in a chair in the sand reading Eknath Easwaran's *Conquest of Mind*. I was scrambling like a mad dog to get a grip on my own thoughts and feelings, and I felt sure that book would help. It did, but not in any way I expected. Part of me wanted to just party on, ignoring the feelings I was fighting. That book taught me to recognize the power of my own thoughts and how to dip below the tumultuous surface to a deeper place within me. The thoughts and feelings didn't go away, but I was slowly becoming able to sort out some of them – some, not all.

There I sat, the former merrymaker with her nose in a book about changing her thoughts through meditation. Talk about a screaming red flag that something was amiss! If any of the group asked me why I was reading that kind of book, I don't remember. Probably a good thing. What could I have possibly said? "Well, I've been feeling lonely here with all of you around me in this beautiful setting, so I thought I'd try to figure out why." Oh, brother. Talk about being loosely woven.

It was in those moments that I initiated the construction of a different sort of relationship with myself and with powers beyond my then understanding. Over time my constant seeking stopped feeling so "sinful." The "God" I used to fear took the form of everything around me, not the man who had an opinion about my every move. The judgement I imagined I deserved showed itself as my own reflection in a mirror. The exhilaration of knowing there were options in what I chose to believe sent me flying. The flight was both invigorating and harrowing, mostly harrowing for quite a while. I unearthed deep roots of belief knowing there was buried treasure in there somewhere. Kinda like that story of the optimistic twin brother. You know that one?

Twin brothers, and their parents were concerned they had developed extreme personality characteristics. One an extreme pessimist and the other an extreme optimist. The psychologist they chose decided to treat the pessimist first. He showed the child to a room filled floor to ceiling with toys, hoping the kid would jump for joy. Nope. He immediately began to cry, complaining that soon the batteries in the toys would die, and he would surely break them if he played with them.

The psychologist then took the optimistic child to a room filled floor to ceiling with horse manure. That child leaped gleefully onto the pile. He slugged his way to the top and began to dig into it with his bare hands, shouting, "With this much poop, there's sure to be a pony in here somewhere!"

I would love to tell you that it all happened overnight. That a few weeks or months fixed it all, but that would be stretching the truth beyond recognition. Over twenty years later, and meditation still feels sweet to me. It has taken many forms, depending on the day, and on the best days feels like I've dropped my butt down on a dirt path in the middle of a garden of wild flowers. Heaven on earth for me.

I now have Christian friends who snicker when I use the words "Universe" or "Source" and New Thought friends who do the same when I say "God" or "Jesus." Why does it have to be "either or?" Can't it be "both and?" Is there only one way to find inner peace? The key word is "peace." Not *righteousness,* or *whatever.* Neither of those words is based in love. I'm proposing a personal tranquility that underlies the agitations of our universal culture. A serenity that may get fluffed up at times, but can withstand the louder voices of those determined to convince otherwise. For me, daily meditation allowed for deep mining.

The words I chose for my foray into meditation included the line on my father's gravestone, "It is in dying that we are born to eternal life." *The Prayer of Saint Francis* was one of my dad's favorites, and the words brought me a modicum of peace.

Make me a channel of your peace.
Where there is hatred let me sow love.
Where there is injury, pardon.

Where there is doubt, faith.
Where there is despair, hope.
Where there is darkness, light.
Where there is sadness, joy.

Oh, Master grant that I may never seek
So much to be consoled as to console,
To be understood as to understand,
To be loved as to love with all my soul.

For it is in giving that we receive.
It is in pardoning that we are pardoned.
And it's in dying that we're born to eternal life.

I repeated those verses over and over as my universe spun out of control. I still believe today that those words held my spirit to my body. I somehow knew there was life yet to be lived, although I also felt within a hair's breadth of choosing to leave my body behind.

If you know of Louise Hay, you know of her study of the body and how it is impacted by our thoughts, leading to our emotions. Her book *You Can Heal Your Life*, came to me through a dear friend who had also taken a divergent path. I had only begun to understand the implications of my own thinking when I broke my foot playing volleyball and was told my bones were thinning. Well, *ain't that somethin'*? I smile now when I look at the emotional foundation for those two events! Louise's book, which I have now carried in my purse for over 20 years, states, in the column next to "Broken bones", "Rebelling against authority and mental pressures, loss of mental mobility." Yep! That was me! I had decided nobody was ever again going to tell me what to do, and the mental stress of isolation was deadly.

What doesn't kill you makes you stronger, right? Apparently, but the strength may not be perceivable in the moment.

Meditation on Isolation

As I continued to make overtures to my family in an attempt to open a slammed door, I also attempted to "play normal." My daughter and I went to ball games and built forts in the living room. She and I occasionally slept outside on the deck with our dog Nelly, dragging our mattresses out the back door along with the bedding. I was conscious enough to know that I wanted to soak up the joy of every moment with her.

During the holidays of the first year after divorcing, I purchased a Christmas tree and spent all night decorating it to surprise my daughter in the morning. I fell into bed around 2:30 a.m., awoke later in the morning, made my way down the hall to the living room, and found the tree lying on the carpet, bulbs and lights everywhere. Unable to lift it by myself, I called for help, but was refused.

"Nope. You can handle it yourself." Click. Again, I crumbled in a heap to the carpet. I wished there were a hatch in the floor that I could fall through and never be seen again. My skin barely contained the emotions that were exploding inside. Why did I keep being surprised at the responses I received? Was it simply the shock of having gone from *cherished* to *despised*? I recalled my childhood memories of those families left behind as they walked out of the funeral home to continue living and wondered at that moment, "*Why bother?*"

Tearfully, I removed all the decorations from the tree and somehow lifted it back into its stand. By the time my daughter awoke the tree was shining beautifully in the front window. They were right. I *could* handle it myself — without them. Not my first choice, but one that had been made for me. Or so I believed at the time.

My need to understand those who held my heart in their hands was equal to my need to understand myself. What the hell was wrong with me? Why couldn't I hold on to what I had been taught? How did I ever become so self-centered and unwilling to accept things as they were? Who was I to throw everyone else into a tailspin? If their intention was to punish me to death, they came mighty close to just that. I was lambasted by their retaliation, and at the same time felt I deserved every bit of it. There was nowhere to turn but inside, and the guilt and shame I found there was colossal.

What had happened to that lighthearted yet sensible and fun-loving girl who was once the life of the party? These words were written in a letter from my niece some 3 years after my divorce. She and I had been more like sisters, and by the time her words reached me I was barely breathing, incapable of revisiting what had happened in that life. The torch that had lit the pyre of my previous existence could not have burned hotter than my own self-judgment. I was pretty convinced that I wasn't worthy of the life I had been granted. Would I ever recover from the guilt I felt for causing such family sorrow? I had known I was uneasy inside the life I had, but hadn't foreseen the upheaval my choices would induce.

I had flashbacks of time spent with family and friends. Some of my favorite times were spent on my bicycle with our rider group. We cycled hundreds of miles preparing for weeklong rides alongside thousands of others through Ohio and Iowa. I wore a big yellow helmet and was the slowest one in the pack... always last to come in. The husbands in our group rode ahead of us at their own pace. One day, after covering 100 miles, I crawled in through the fairground gate, barely upright in my seat. My husband was standing there waiting. He had been worried since it had begun to get dark. He said to me, "If I rode as slowly as you do, I'd fall off my bike! There's barely enough forward momentum to keep you going!" I was so darned tired, and I took offense to his comment. Looking back, it makes me laugh. He was right. I was a snail.

The next day we started out again, and eventually, we girls had to make a pit stop in one of the local corn fields. We each picked our row in the field and went in, carrying our rolls of toilet paper with us. After we finished we all got back on our bikes to continue on, focused on our goal. Pulling up the rear gave me the advantage that day. We had not gone 50 feet before I saw it, and I nearly fell over when I did. One of my companions was riding along unaware that a corn stalk from the field was riding with her. It was stuck in the back of her spandex shorts and flying high in the breeze over her back wheel. I shouted, and we all had to stop before we hurt ourselves laughing.

I missed them all, and years went by. While participating in a 60-mile 3-day walk a new friend handed me several CDs with presentations by someone named Abraham Hicks. This precious friend had somehow figured that I would appreciate the content. Those CDs landed like spring rain on dry soil. Yep! I was living proof that what I choose to think about and put my attention on gets me more of just *that*. I had spent the previous several years focusing intently on my victimhood, guilt and anger and all the time wondering why my life still felt like the ruins of an ancient castle. I hadn't comprehended how my own thoughts and emotions were primary contributors to my sense of isolation. If I could have abandoned my own ship, I would have. No wonder everyone else had. In my own mind I was pitiful and undeserving as a result of what I had chosen to do. Who wants to hang out with that person?

Grief held me like a baby in its arms. Why live, if those I loved had decided to quit the game? The mornings were the worst. I just wanted to stay asleep so I didn't have to think. The minute my eyes opened I began to cry. Classic signs of depression, right? The bottom had fallen out. How would I ever be able to move forward? Who would love me? Did I have any purpose at all? Where was my confidence? Would I ever be close to my family again? Could we laugh together again? Would the fucking elephant that was sitting on my chest ever stand the hell up so I could breathe? I didn't know. I needed to look ahead, but I couldn't see past whatever day it was.

Explaining myself to me was nearly impossible, and it would be years before I recognized the strength that was growing from all my unanswered prayers. I read and listened to dozens of philosophies. If an idea resonated, I held onto it. If it sounded like bullshit, I threw it out. Some of my favorites were approaches I really wanted to believe, but they still sounded like potential bullshit. Take the idea of God being non-judgmental. Yup! Loved *that* idea, but I just couldn't get the picture of the man with the beard out of my head.

What did I do with that one? I hung a poster in my mind about it, read all kinds of writings on the definition of "God," checked in with my own feeling about the concept, listened to preachers, gurus, former priests, and finally let it take up residence inside. The joy of the process began to intrigue me. The new thoughts, invited to complete an internship with me, slowly edged out the old. Over time I laid a new foundation one belief at a time, and I know completing the structure will be a lifelong endeavor.

I sometimes wonder, looking back, how it took me so darned long to figure out that some of what I claimed to believe as a young person really wasn't what I believed at all. I guess I had never thought about it. I had sat at family dinners listening to the conversation and had felt a twinge of disagreement with what's being said, but decided to keep my mouth shut because I didn't want to ruffle feathers or appear to be disrespectful.

I did everything I knew to mask my growing desperation. Remember high school pep rallies? Everyone's screaming and shouting for the home team. No one can know you have a secret crush on one of the players on the other side. "Go defense!!" Maybe cheering louder will throw others off your scent.

I executed that game plan by using my Catholic beliefs. Feeling despondent led me to dive into my faith. I prayed hundreds of rosaries, attended Mass at every opportunity, lit candles. I even made the traditional pilgrimage on my knees with hundreds of others from the church plaza to Mary's altar at a cathedral high in the mountains of Latin America. I didn't know what to do with my life, and so as a symbolic gesture I left my rosary on that altar, praying that God would handle things for me, since I felt I couldn't.

Most of the people around me claimed to believe the same stuff I was taught to believe, so there was no doubt that had something to do with my reticence. I guess timing is everything, as they say.

Expanding My Mind Frame

Several months after abandoning my marriage, a dear friend and I were browsing the shelves of a local bookstore. This particular friend had spent years studying Catholicism, the history of the Mystics, and had a Master's degree in Creation

Spirituality. Once upon a time she had been a student in my classroom and had grown into an influential, heart-centered woman. I respected her journey and sought her input. My world had just crumbled around me, and I was asking for guidance. Little did I know it would come that day. As I was scanning an upper stack, my friend reached to pull a book from a shelf at my knees, waved it up behind her so I could see it, and said, "Straub, read this book. It will change your life."

That moment and that book rocked my world. The contents were so apart from what I had ever considered possible that I clearly remember reading one section at a time, laying it face down on the coffee table, and saying out loud to myself, "Oh, shit. Really?" I'd stand up, wander the same pattern throughout the house and then return to my seat attempting to steady my nervous system as it absorbed the implications of the information that book held for me.

All I could hear was "Heard It Through the Grapevine" by Marvin Gaye. "People say believe half of what you see, Son, and none of what you hear." What I saw on those pages had me swinging through the trees in my mind. It was a wild ride that thrilled me to the core. Do I believe everything I read? Of course not. Yet you and I can both recognize, if we choose to, that feeling we get in our solar plexus the minute a piece of information rings true for us. The contents of that book rang true for me. I circled that coffee table and wore a path in the carpet down my hall trying to find a place to settle my mind and heart. I'm now grateful there were no cameras to record my up-down-around-straight-then back again to the couch trail. There might have been room for some misinterpretation standing on the outside looking in. The book I was reading was *Many Lives, Many Masters,* by Dr. Brian Weiss.

Dr. Weiss is a psychiatrist who in 1980 was Chief of Psychiatry at Mount Sinai Medical Center in Miami. At the time, he was challenged in treating one of his patients, "Catherine." Eventually, this patient began relating her experiences from other lifetimes, but at the time Dr. Weiss did not buy the notion of past lives or reincarnation. His view began to change after he confirmed details from Catherine's accounts through historical records. After more sessions he also noticed that the experience of past life regression had a positive effect on Catherine's health, as well as the health of his other patients. Eventually, he chose to go public with his findings, and now he travels the world doing workshops and seminars explaining his approach. His workshops are both mind-bending and fascinating.

What? I might have been here before, and may come again as someone else later (assuming one believes in linear time)? That's just ridiculous. There is no way! Oh no! The Church is clearly not in favor of that concept! This is the second time I've come across this idea, and both sources are well-educated, highly-accomplished physicians. The tug-of-war between the thrill of possibilities and the need to hold onto my old beliefs made my mind and body ache. I was sure my parents, priests, and nuns would not have agreed with that twisted notion, and I had only recently begun to consider it myself. I'd like to say I would have quoted the Bible here for evidence against reincarnation, but the truth was, after sixteen years of Catholic school education I couldn't have quoted a single scripture from the Bible.

My wonderful religion teachers did their best with me on this, and I was a good student. I passed all their tests. I recited the Ten Commandments, answered the questions posed by the Baltimore Catechism, and told short stories from the Bible like a pro. As I write this I realize that I can still recite many of the answers we memorized. Past conditioning can be like riding a bike. Wow. A lot of what they taught me I learned to believe, and there are pieces I still do. I even continued to get all puffed up, *after* having left the Church, when someone challenged a Catholic stance. How could anyone believe otherwise? Most of me was so darned sure. And now, here I was, standing at a crossroads, challenging myself. Of course, in the beginning of this journey I didn't say much because that would have been disrespectful or outright heretical. To pose that God was something or someone other than what we saw on our holy cards could get me after school detention at the very least. I never tested that supposition. I just kind of knew it. I think the voice of "maybe not" was at first little like the little girl I was, and grew with me as I grew up.

My mother was the only one who ever heard me argue against any of the Church's dogma, and she made it clear my voicing it was only asking for trouble. Church doctrine had an answer to every challenging question. Why fast before receiving Holy Communion? So, your body was pure to receive the body of Christ. Why did the bishop have to give us a little slap when we were confirmed? To prove that we were "soldiers for Christ." Why did we have to give up something for Lent every year? To practice the art of self-denial. Looking back, I now believe I might have made her a little crazy with all of my questions, and she did her best to keep me on the straight and narrow for my own good, fearing one day I might break loose and really mess up the works. Eventually, I did and I did. And I will be forever grateful to myself that I did.

Know this. Once a long-held belief gets a hair thin crack in it, your system may become wobbly. You may want to run for the hills and never come back. You may find yourself stuttering as you try to explain your thoughts out loud to yourself. Fear not! Those are the rickety feelings of growth happening. It may be uncomfortable, but you'll most likely live through it. And when you come out the other end, you might feel the power of your own spirit. Why? Because what you traversed was the pathway to your own belief system. Yea you!

I recognized I had deeply held beliefs. I later came to recognize I had never questioned the foundation of those beliefs. What I'm discussing here are concepts we adopt as children, live with through the decades of our lives and never investigate. Could the investigation become uncomfortable? Yep. Eventually, after continuing to challenge my own foundation, I alighted much like a helicopter, on a landing pad with a big red "X" meant just for me. Touching down on my "X" I felt much like I did stepping across the threshold of my brand-new home. I knew it was where I belonged. I took my time. It was not possible to rush the process anyway. I rested for a bit, enjoyed and appreciated the gift I had given myself. Once I opened the door of possibility, that "X" was only one of many I learned to appreciate. I landed, got comfortable, delighted in my new discoveries, and then began again. Being a creative creature, as we all are, I am loving my new *home* and still ready for more. There's always more. That flexibility allows me space to breathe in the nuances of this life.

The Guilt Wrapped Up in Giving

I outlined the picture of my blessed and beautiful childhood. Somewhere in there I learned to believe that if I had too much, then someone else must be doing without. That was my interpretation, and I'm pretty certain my parents had the same unconscious guilt. There was some sort of sanctity in not having too many material goods. I have always felt grateful for what I had, and have wanted to give wherever I could, yet there was a certain amount of guilt wrapped up in my giving. As if my giving could make up for the fact that someone else had less than I did. Kinda like that cherry pie that has only a certain number of pieces, and if I take more than my share, then you're outta luck.

The concept of our compassionately caring for one another with the understanding that our good fortune is not taking away from someone else's came to me much later. As I learned more about the limitless universe and my place in it, I slowly released the chains that had bound my sense of deserving. My certainty that I deserved to be punished held fast. I didn't want to have too much for fear that the other shoe would drop. All of it would probably get ripped out from under me again. As I studied the ideas of a boundless world and a god that held no judgement, the links in those chains loosened. I recognized that my having joy did not take away from another person having the same. In fact, my having more joy might very well bring more joy to those around me. Now there's a concept! I had to really run that one through the wringer before I could shake it out. My earning a good income and living in a lovely home did not reduce the chances for someone else. Remember guilt? The gift that keeps on giving!

Anything we tell ourselves enough times eventually becomes a belief. We can get frozen in our beliefs, never venturing out to see if the world really is flat. What if? That question can clear pathways in our mind we never imagined existed. Pathways to awareness and joy, acceptance and love. Asking ourselves "what if" in an effort to broaden our experience will keep our childlike curiosity forever wanting more. The thrill of self-discovery is unlike any other. One word of caution; Using that same question to terrorize our-selves is harrowing and self-defeating in every way imagin-able. I do my best to stay conscious of the direction in which I'm pointing my "what if" arrow. A poor aim can easily lead to my "catastrophizing." Example: What if Chicken Little *was* right about the sky falling?

The following "what ifs" and resulting conclusions still lift my heart. You may agree with my conclusions or not. It's ok either way. Remember, this "choosing" what to believe is exactly that. A choice.

What if… my gods have no opinion or judgement at all about what we do or say, and are simply the power of love flowing in and through everything and everyone? Anything deemed "evil" is more an indication of our conscious dis-connection from Infinite Spirit than an entity out to get us? What if heaven and hell are both here in our earthly experi-ence, and not destinations determined by the man on the bench? Is it possible we are simply here to experience life in this form and any heaven or hell we live is of our own making right here? Could we be in this form now, and when we die, there's really no place to go because we are always everywhere? We simply put down our current body in favor of living an experience of pure love? And any final judge-ment story was something made-up centuries ago by men wanting to control the masses?

If God truly is omniscient, omnipotent, and omnipres-ent, then why do we shy away from the less formal interpre-tations of those three words — all-knowing, all-powerful, and present everywhere? It seems to me that as believers, we are comfortable with the *all-knowing* and *all-powerful* concepts, but cherry-pick the idea of *present everywhere in everything.* "Surely, God is not present in the terrorist or in the concrete sidewalk outside my house." If I believe God to embody those three traits, then God is not only *out there somewhere* but *in* me *as* me. For me, Source, God, Universal Energy is a life force present in every human, tree, rock, animal, no matter what their earth suit looks like, sounds like, or does. If we believe that, then where did we learn to anthropomorphize that love force, and why would it ever condemn *itself* to the everlasting fires of Hell? If God is in me, and I go to Hell, doesn't God go with me? Or is there a *God-stop*, where God gets off the bus before reaching the final destination? For me, the idea that God judges us is an egocentric construct conceived by humans living in fear of losing control. My choices create my own heaven or hell as I walk through my day.

Those concepts can really mess with my mind and my studying their possibilities removed more fear and anxiety than I realized I had. Whoa! Talk about rattling the cage! The releasing of certain foundational creeds allowed me to breathe in as if standing on a mountain top, free from an underlying energy or fear of "The Guy in the Sky." If the essence of God or Source is pure love, and I am powered by that love, then I am the one who gets to decide how this is going to play out, knowing that my conscious connection to that source energy is of quintessential importance. I also recognized the potential challenges of holding these beliefs. Previous conditioning and current cultural mores were and are powerful influencers.

What if... all of our experiences on the outside are merely a result of what we have been thinking about and feeling on the inside? Over and over again? In other words, what if things don't happen to us. What if they happen *through* us, and our attitudes and ideas are what bring us into line with what we live out every day? Not the random hand of a sometimes benevolent, sometimes vengeful God?

So, changing those ideas about our life's happenings can change the future happenings? Staying conscious of and intentionally adjusting my perspective and attitude will result in something other than what I have known in the past? I say, "Yes."

What if … we chose to believe that all of us can be healthy up to our last breath? That we don't need to get sick before we die, we just step out of our bodies when the time is right and go on to the next experience? I realize that would really screw up the commercials we see during the nightly news, but I'd be ok with that. Maybe our emotions have more to do with our illnesses than any germ. Maybe we've watched so many loved ones suffer through illnesses that we have come to accept the inevitability of our experiencing it too. Could we Baby Boomers have one more revolution left in us? That of "Happy, Healthy, Dead?" I heard Ester Hicks say that once, and it has always stuck with me. Who needs *sick* first? Scientists are now all in on the idea of the mind/body connection and the power of the mind to heal the body. Another component to that is the power of our emotions to create/heal our illnesses.

As I mentioned earlier, my explorations led me to Louise Hay, the author of *You Can Heal Your Life*. I just referenced this barn burner of a book twice today. Because of her experiences Louise connected the emotions we feel to the sicknesses we experience, and for me that connection has proven fully reliable. When I find myself under the weather for any reason, I pull out the book and search for what might be going on in my own head. I'd like to say that I am fully conscious of my every thought, but that would be grossly overestimating myself. I may not particularly appreciate what I read, but it's likely the truth of the matter. I can then address it.

Believe It and See It

What if … we really could be, do, have all that we wanted to, and all it took was our increasing our ability to *believe* that? Now that could be a lot of fun!

If we have the courage and willingness to begin to challenge any of our previously held beliefs, where do we begin to find those that may not be serving us? I'd like to say, "Be observant," but I can't claim that I was. I was living my beautiful life, loving most of it, and ignoring the occasional tap on the shoulder. It wasn't until the taps became a freight train blaring its whistle that I really considered making a move. I finally recognized that I had more days of feeling "off" than "on." On my birthday I heard myself complaining about the gift my husband had given me. The feelings I had were shocking *me*. What the hell was my problem? Who complains about a gift? Although my anger and frustration were not always outwardly expressed, those feelings buzzed in my head like a neon sign with *WTF* flashing twenty-four seven.

I noticed I was just feeling cranky for no apparent reason. There was a reason alright. I was thinking something I was not even aware of. I was so good at doing the immediate cover-up, I didn't even know when one or more of my thoughts had taken me hostage. I was just plain annoyed all the time at every little thing. Examples? A co-worker made a joke I didn't like, or my husband shrank something in the dryer, or one of my kids gave me a disapproving glance. These weren't war initiatives, just little pin pricks that I wasn't tuned in to. Next thing I knew I was snapping at the dog for looking at me with his head cocked sideways.

The most insidious of these little dive bombers was resentment. Every little aggravation became a story I held onto for dear life. I'd rehearse the feelings of those stories over and over in my head, justifying myself all day long and silently rehearsing the sermons I'd really like to deliver, once given the chance. The days became weeks and then months. Is there a story you're still holding on to, and although it's a perfectly beautiful day in the neighborhood, you find yourself getting snarky with the girl in the drive-through because she put too much cream in your coffee? You think she and the cream are the culprits for your frustration, but maybe not.

With me there's always something under the current agitation that is the true offender, and sometimes it pays to figure out what that is before I go any further in my day. It can be a small irksome moment from this morning at breakfast. Maybe it's the fear I felt when the school called to say my child was sick. Maybe it's the frustration I felt when my boss corrected my report yesterday. Simply looking at it may be enough to let it go right then and there. Sometimes it takes longer. I say, *sometimes*, because I have since learned it does me no good to relive the past. I am more likely to snap out of it, if I recognize my current feelings and then choose to focus on thoughts that lift my spirits. Thinking of my cute dog or my good health can often do the trick. Sometimes it takes longer. Here's one of my observations of *me* that has stayed with me for a long time. Maybe it will help you.

One evening my 10-year-old daughter and I were in the kitchen. I asked her to empty the dishwasher, and she made it clear to me that she didn't want to. At that moment I got angry, raised my voice, and sent her to her room (or something like that... it was 20 years ago). I now recognize that I had a belief at the time that said, "If you are a good mother, MaryBob, your child will do what you tell her. So, if your children are *not* doing what you tell them, then you must be a bad mother." Add to that, "What will your friends and neighbors think of *you* if your child does not behave? Both you and I know that what others think of you is of paramount importance in determining your value as a human being." Keep in mind, her older brother had done more than his share of *not* doing what we told him, so I may have been a bit overly sensitive.

Don't get flustered here and think that I've mastered the art of instantaneously recognizing my own digressions. My logical brain did not come up with all of that on the spot. None of that stuff even occurred to me until years later, when I first ventured into the realm of "What do I really believe?" I have to say though, the recognition of that one little thing has helped me ease into my own self more than I can express here. After that realization, I felt much like I suppose an archeologist feels upon the discovery of one small shard of ancient pottery. Bring in more tools! This *dig* has only just begun!

With the passing of time I have formed the habit of stepping back when I feel a negative emotion and asking myself two questions; What am I afraid of? What am I believing right now that's giving me this crappy feeling? You may want to try this too, the next time you catch yourself feeling *off* or outright ballistic about something. I began asking myself where I had learned my beliefs, since I'm certain I wasn't born with them. How does that belief make me feel? Self-righteous? Compassionate? Does that belief open my heart to the world around me, or does it feel constricting? Let me say here, that this has been, and still is, a process. I suspect the process will continue until I take my last breath. I'm happy about that. This is a prime example of, "It's not about being perfect. It's about making progress." As my husband says, "Perfection precludes evolution. I *am* perfect in my Divine essence and therefore, even with my flaws, and in my human-ness I am always growing, evolving." Maybe there are other beliefs that you've been curious about, but up 'til now seemed too far out to consider viable. Here are a couple of my own that I unearthed along the way;

At one time, I thought arranged marriages were borderline ridiculous. Then, once again, my curiosity got me going, so I decided, for graduate school research, to interview couples whose marriages had originated in exactly that manner. My eyes, brain and heart were thrown open by the beauty of what I learned. Yes, their marriages were arranged, but with the couples I interviewed, the arrangement had both of their consents in advance. They had grown in love for each other over time, much like Tevye and Golde in "Fiddler on the Roof." The divorce rate for arranged marriages? Six percent in the most recent study I found. I am obviously not anti-divorce, but six percent beats the hell out of our current 55% for "Will you marry me?" marriages. Yes, there are most likely some *arranged* couples who would be better off divorced, but it's a long hike from 6% to 55%. Think of the time, money and sorrow saved in that cultural practice.

Here's another one I thought was nonsense. Energy healing. What the heck is that all about? You people are nut cakes. Wouldn't a capsule of medicine be an easier solution? My previous life had been filled to the brim with conventional Western medicine, and it, no doubt, has its place in healing. Yet, over the years I've seen more than my share of friends and family feel so much better after a consultation with focused energy. Maybe it simply depends on what we believe to be true. There is so much we don't know. What have I learned? There is some truth in every approach, every religion, every philosophy. It's my job to put together my own house.

For me, the concepts of my truth are mine and mine alone. If I choose to appropriate a "universal" truth as my own, that is my option. As Henry Ford once said, "Whether you think you can or think you can't, you're right." So why not think I *can* be, do, have the dreams of this lifetime? More importantly, once examined and appropriated by me, I feel no need to defend it. Since I've taken the time to look closely at it, I am peaceful in the midst of others who may disagree. They have their options, and I have mine. When I observe another defending his/her beliefs with anger and harshness, I tend to think they are feeling the need to convince *themselves* more than anyone else. For me, a belief held in love does not require defense, particularly when the defense mechanism results in attacking another for her truth. Expressions such as, "Ye shall not enter the kingdom of heaven" or "Hell awaits those who sin," do not, in my opinion, come from the love of God. They are judgement. And why the need to shout? If those statements are true for the speaker, wouldn't it be enough to state them in an "indoor voice?" I thought shouting was best used outdoors. At least that's what my mother used to tell me.

Can you imagine a world filled with varying beliefs joyfully expanding and accepted? In this world there would be no need to argue. If someone else's belief does not resonate with me, then I simply "turn the other cheek." I can appreciate the walk they're taking, acknowledge their expression, if I sense they need to feel heard, and then choose to lay my focus on what feels peaceful to me. If each belief were deeply excavated and found to be based in love not fear, would we not live in peace? I often wonder if we would need prisons if each person took the time to explore and come to peace with themselves. For me it's the inner battle that results in the outer altercation. I'm aware that sounds lofty, so no need to email me on that one. We can all start somewhere, right?

Back to the story….

Over two years passed and no change. Family celebrations came and went. Eventually, I was invited back to my seat at the table, but it was not the same. More often than not the room went silent as I walked in the back door — the air holding skeletal lines of conversation. "Anybody know where the electric knife is?" The best person for me to talk to was my ten-year-old daughter. The shoes I was wearing were painful, but at that point I didn't know how to shake them off my feet.

A few people with whom I had communicated before the big event came out of the woodwork, but the temperature of my former relationships never rose above freezing. I was, honest to God, shocked beyond measure. I mean, if I'd put a beef roast in the freezer and left it there that long, it would have had a serious case of freezer burn. Inedible and irretrievable, and that's exactly what happened in my own mind. Throw that sucker away 'cuz there ain't no point in trying to revive a dead horse. Do your best to get your shit together, and move on. I really did want to stop the world and step off, but into what?

OUTTA DODGE

"When we are no longer able to change a situation, we are challenged to change ourselves."
– Viktor Frankl

The Pathway that Opened for Me

Kicking the tumbleweeds down the dusty streets of my previous life gave me lots of opportunities to evaluate. I'm not saying I was clear in my thinking, but I am saying I had made one definite decision. My gold mine had run dry, and the sheriff was crooked. It was up to me to make a change. This skeleton of a life was *not* going to push me into my next incarnation. I was not ready to be a corpse like those I had seen lying in caskets in my parent's funeral home. My two children were not going to grow up without me, so now, after some serious considerations and having chosen to continue to live, I found myself at a crossroads — not consciously, but I was definitely at a turning point. Something beyond my comprehension was moving me while I was out to lunch.

Here's how it went…

About a year after my divorce I received an issue of my favorite magazine *Common Boundary*. It was a periodical that elaborated on the growing relationship between science and spirituality. I soaked it up looking for answers to my own conundrum. Within the pages of this particular issue was a post card advertising an organization in California called The Empowerment Learning Institute. I was already making monthly pilgrimages to Oakland, CA to study at The University of Creation Spirituality, so California made sense to me. Matthew Fox had founded this school after being excommunicated from the Catholic Church, which gave him credibility for me at the time, and I found his teachings to be another avenue for my ever-growing need for expansion.

ELI was looking for facilitators for its program in emotion education. I was a school teacher after all, and boy, did I ever have emotions! I might even be an expert by now. Little did I know. One more way to work on myself to maintain my sanity. I signed up and began my distance learning with them. I faltered and eventually got back in the saddle a year later. Over that year nothing had improved in Dodge. My lifeline was thinning, and I was witnessing my own demise.

Sharing the parenting of our daughter left me ample opportunity to be alone with my thoughts – a dangerous place. Friday afternoons were the pits. School over, my daughter at her dad's house, me sitting in the garage listening to the garage door drop, wondering how I was going to make it through the night. I knew I had to get my thinking under control. I knew that passing the hours revisiting visions of long-ago weekends spent with family and friends was not helping my emotional state. Despite anti-depressants and therapy sessions, I was still trying to determine how to get out of my body *alive*, but gone – anywhere where this life *wasn't*. My therapist along with the few family and friends still standing knew I had fallen off my horse, been trampled, and the buzzards were circling.

One particular Friday, the panic in my chest was rising fast, so I called my sister, who then lived about an hour away.

She got in her car and showed up at my front door bearing gifts — 3 Xanax tablets. I resisted, but she insisted I take *half* of one of those tablets, and thank God, I followed her directive. Once I calmed down she sat beside me on the couch and read out loud to me, forcing my mind to go somewhere else, her hand covering mine. I breathed.

She listened to me cry, and simply took my face in her hands to say, "I'm here, and I'm not leaving you." My body continued to show the wear of the upheaval. It seemed that every few weeks I was taking a new medication for some ailment I had never before experienced. I think I was the poster child for depression.

Even teaching could not hold my attention. I loved my "kids" so, but the personal fog was too thick to see through. My mother-in-law, as confused as the rest of the world, confronted me as I got out of my car at school one morning. She wanted to know why I was making the choice I was. The principal saw us standing in the parking lot, and held my class until I could gather myself enough to stand in front of the room. Twenty years earlier I had made a pact with myself. I had noticed a few teachers in the teacher's lounge counting down their years to retirement, and I decided I was not going to do that. I told myself then that if I ever stopped loving my life in the classroom, I would quit because it wasn't fair for the kids to be learning from someone who no longer held the passion to teach. The pain I was experiencing was affecting my teaching, so after twenty years in the classroom, I submitted my resignation without any idea what to do next.

At that point it had been two years since my divorce, and my relationship with my mother was cordial at best. I announced to her that I had resigned from teaching, and no wonder she thought I was nuts. She was eighty-four years old, and her youngest child's mind had just flown the coop. How was I going to support myself and my daughter? I didn't know, and I didn't much care. I just knew I could not go on as I had.

Fortunately, ELI had a weeklong workshop that summer in Chicago, and I was still receiving a paycheck from the school system, so I decided to attend. Bill, who is now my husband, then worked for ELI. He arranged for me to room with his former wife since she was a high school counselor, and I was a teacher. He figured we'd have a lot in common. Little did Bill know *he* would be the biggest part of what we had in common. More on that later. For me there was nothing to lose. Literally nothing. I drove there in tears, praying that I would once again feel blood running in my veins. It had been too long since the door had been locked on the cooler. Someway, somehow, I was determined to taste sweetness again. What I experienced there put me on a life-giving course. That week led me to individuals who were seekers like me, and they didn't have any attachment to how I showed up. The only baggage I had with them was what I brought with me in my own mind. The founder was direct and somewhat blunt, and I could have gotten my feelings hurt, but he was exactly what the doctor ordered. He told it like it was, and more than that he gave me inspiration for the possibility of life renewed.

He and his beautiful wife talked to us about "Life Scripts." You know, those not-so-precious recordings that constantly run in our heads about how we are "less than." The over-arching script is "There is something wrong with me." The variations on that theme are: "I am not good enough," "I don't belong," and my personal favorites, "I did something wrong," and "I deserve to be punished." These two gems were my constant companions at the time. I'm thinking we've all had a conversation or two with these *lovelies* at one time or another. The realization that these thoughts had been scampering around in my brain was life-altering. I learned how emotions and thoughts are all tied up together, and that with focus and attention I can undo those knots. We discussed different approaches to spirituality and how our beliefs impacted our current life situations. The days were filled with ideas for discussion and tools to use on the path toward self-appreciation and acceptance. For me it was veritable feast.

In the evenings we were asked to stay silent to assimilate what we had learned and begin to "know" our spiritual selves. We each found a nook in the monastery and sat with our workbooks, processing what we had absorbed that day. It's a darned good thing I had been on the meditation trail at that point because that might have driven me to drink! As it turned out I loved every minute of it. It was as if someone had thrown me a lifeline, and I had finally been able to grasp the end of it. I might have been gulping all sorts of water at the time, but I had determined I wasn't going to drown. This rescue effort may not be pretty, but I had finally found some sense of direction.

Do I Stay or Do I Go?

We all have difficult decisions to make at times. *Not* making a decision can make us crazy, and I was already that, so do I go or do I stay? Do I leave what I've known my whole life for a shot at something I felt might possibly be more expansive or do I stay here and try for another "who-knows-how-many years" to patch things up? Do I leave my young daughter or do I stay for her sake, knowing I was barely hanging on to the "good mother" medal as it was? What am I teaching her, if I go? What am I teaching her, if I stay? Who really cares if

I go or stay? A post-it note could hold the names in response to that last question. What about my mom? What about my house? What about my car? What about my declining health? How am I going to support myself? Jesus, Mary, and Joseph, the list of questions was endless, and the answers were preposterous. At the time, I believed I could be damned if I did and damned if I didn't. Yep, I was damned no matter what, so I took a shot in the dark hoping to at least land on the board alive somewhere.

There really wasn't anyone to get input from, so I just decided to go. You know how the cowboy just rides out of the dusty town at the end of a western movie? I wasn't much good with horses, so a plane would have to do. There weren't a lot of arrangements to be made. Call the realtor, buy a ticket, sell everything I owned, somehow tell my daughter and mother (let's not relive those moments), hand in my car, get a ride to the airport and poof! I'm gone. There ya go! Thank God for autopilot because the controller had lost control, and the air inside my cabin was mighty thin. The only available oxygen mask stretched to me from California.

BEFORE IT GETS BETTER

"You may encounter many defeats, but you must not be defeated. In fact, it may be necessary to encounter the defeats, so you can know who you are, what you can rise from, how you can still come out of it."
– Maya Angelou

Exodus from Pleasantville

Making the decision to exit stage left was one thing. Executing that idea was something else. My once-protective cocoon had grown dry and crusty, and I was shriveling up inside. Somehow, I had to slide out one of the fissures and make my way toward life. My lungs hadn't felt a deep intake of air in over two years. Something simply had to give.

My only real concerns at that point were my 84-year-old mother and my 11-year-old daughter. Although my mother and I hadn't really had much of a relationship since my divorce, she still had been my best friend and confidant for most of my life, and I adored her. I was yet to recognize the depth of her confusion, so we both nested ourselves in our anger and outrage. Part of me said, "What difference does it make if I leave? We don't talk anymore anyway. She won't even notice, and she has lots of support if she needs something." The other part of me said, "She's 84 years old.

I know she won't understand if I go, and maybe things will get better if I stay a little longer. It's been over two years, but maybe it would be better for me to die here, then everyone can say, 'Poor thing. She just went off the deep end for no reason, and now this. Such a shame'." Upon hearing of my decision to leave, my mother, stunned, simply said she didn't understand. I'm sure she didn't, and I was in no mental or emotional state to try and explain. I just knew I had to go.

Equal to my concern about my mother was that for my 11-year-old daughter. She was the one who had kept me grounded. We had tea parties, campouts, dress-up adventures together, and I couldn't imagine living my life without her. Still, something recognized what a train wreck I was, and I felt incapable of guiding her toward anything positive in life. I asked her if she wanted to go with me, and at first, she said, "Yes." Shortly after, she changed her mind, and I didn't blame her. Both of our families were in that town, all she had ever known. I think she sensed my lack of clarity about what I was doing, and so decided to stay. The thought of leaving her pierced my heart through. She was the only one who could hold me in place. How could I even consider leaving her? What kind of mother does that to her child? I knew. Only the worst kind. And yet staying felt like a self-imposed death sentence. That morning I watched as she walked down the sidewalk to the bus stop in the dark on my last morning in the town I had loved so fiercely, and could barely find my way through my hysteria back inside the house after she turned to wave goodbye. The next four years would be bumpy for both of us, but we learned and grew closer than ever.

Beyond my children, my lifelong friend Debe, two or three others, and some work friends, the rest of my former crowd could all go to hell as far as I was concerned. At that point I couldn't yet see anything but through my own lens. Both of my siblings were still living out of town, but had moved closer than they were earlier, and my former husband was, of course, available to care for my mother, having assumed the permanent role of "second son."

My struggling 22-year-old son lived out of town. Thankfully, I did not have to factor him into my goodbyes. He and I had somehow remained close through his escapades. I can't say I understood what was going on in his head, but since I couldn't understand what was going on in my own head, that was not a shocker. He had recently decided to follow one of his friends out of state, and I was having a venture of my own, so we talked occasionally on the phone. The communication thinned for a year or two while we were both gathering up our "stuff." His world consisted of "work to play," as he says now, and I'm grateful I wasn't witness to all that entailed.

In desperation, I had put prices on yellow sticky notes and pressed them on to every item I owned inside my home. Time to go. My dear friend Maggie, had agreed to hold a garage sale later that week for my possessions, and would send the money to me in California. I locked the side door, got into my Ford Escort, backed out of the driveway, and glanced at the "For Sale" sign in my front yard. I had no intention of taking my car with me, and still owed payments on it, so I headed to the car dealership where I walked through the front door, laid my keys and contact information on the receptionist's counter, turned around and walked out. My forever faithful friend Debe was waiting for me there in her car. She drove my dog and me the seventy-six miles to the Dayton airport where we gave each other a tearful hug. An hour later I boarded a plane to California leaving my so-called life behind. There was only one way my life could go, and that was "up," both literally and figuratively. I learned later that some people in town thought I had joined a cult. After all, it was California, and we all knew what went on there! One local even invented a story about my having called him to request money and rescue from that cult. I guess suspicion was natural for a spectator left sitting in the stands.

I'd like to say I was "present and accounted for" during that time in my life, but I'm certain I was not. The 120-pound body that people addressed as "MaryBob" was the sole remaining artifact of who I had been. I was much like an abandoned house. The plumbing still worked, but my tattered curtains were flapping in breeze, and the floors were rotting. My hands lost their flexibility and strength. My feet tolerated only tennis shoes, and I was told that I habitually walked with my head down. My emotions were blowing through me with such force I could barely stay vertical. My mind-body connection was screaming, and I had only just begun to hear.

California Dreamin'

My new friend Bill from ELI met me at the San Francisco Airport and drove me to the headquarters of ELI. The owners had graciously agreed to my coming shortly after the workshop in Chicago. You know those balloon-like figures that car dealerships put at the street to get your attention? I think I resembled one of those. Pulsating up when the air was flowing and toppling to the ground at the cutoff. I didn't want to feel anything, but what I did feel was profound sorrow, guilt, hurt.

The owners of ELI must have had night vision and through brief conversations determined my pilot light was still lit. Shortly after arriving they both suggested I allow my body the rest it craved and my emotions the outlet they were clamoring for. They prepared a room for me and invited me to stay for "as long as it took." I walked into that room one evening and didn't come out for five days. I ate little and spoke even less, unable to assimilate where I had come from, who I was, and how I expected to move forward. I wrote a complete journal in enormous angry, guilt-induced cursive. I directed my volcanic feelings in every direction until, at last, the flow eased. I felt entirely spent, and somewhat relieved. It would turn out to be the longest, most powerful eruption in my healing. Something had shifted while in that room, and when I came out, I could inhale again.

Those kind souls in that house allowed me to break down to enable the slow process of building up. They fed me, loved me, and held me, a stranger in their midst, because they knew the debilitating power of long held negative emotions and the spiritual connection needed for the maintenance of the human body. They believed I could reconnect, given the time and care, and they were right. My reconstruction had just begun, and although the foundation felt anything but solid, it *was* a foundation.

It was holiday season. Thanksgiving and Christmas were emotional, but I do have a wonderful memory of our time during the holidays in California. Since we lived near Yosemite National Park, the company owners, other workers, Bill and I decided to go ice skating there to celebrate. The breathtaking view of Half Dome made the experience picture-perfect. It was cold, and the sun shone brightly. The new adventure was exhilarating, and the scenery out of this world. Bill, having grown up on the Gulf of Mexico, had little exposure to ice skating. His history of roller skating paid off somewhat, but after spending more time on his butt than on his feet, he decided to use the handrail for support. I'm not a world champion, but had spent many happy hours on ice as a child. Equally exhausted and animated, we had dinner at the beautiful Ahwahnee Hotel nearby. It's now called the Majestic Yosemite Hotel. That experience brought back to me the wonder and awe I had once felt as an adventurer.

Always the Darkest Before the Dawn

Does it really have to get worse before it gets better, or do we just say shit like that because that's what we learned? I mean, yes, in this particular phase of my life it *did* get worse before it got better. I think it did so because I expected it to. I believed I deserved to be punished for any number of things, so it was kind of a self-fulfilling prophecy.

Why do we do that? By "that" I mean "assume the worst." There is no way we come out of the womb thinking that stuff! We learn to be fearful, and then like birds of a feather flocking together, we marvel at it all when it shows up exactly the way we were afraid it just might. That is some kind of crazy right there! Proposition: If we learned it, why can't we unlearn it? Ok, maybe we can't *un*learn something, but I have come to believe we can *re*learn our knee-jerk reactions to what shows up in our lives. Does it take focus and intention day after day after day? Yep! I just kept believing there was another way to live in my skin, and I knew if I searched long enough it would present itself. It did, once piece at a time. One of the most valuable pieces in the puzzle was my learning to create a vision of what I *did* want and spending less time mentally slushing around in what I did *not* want.

So, what if we assumed things would just get better without it getting worse first? I can hear it now...

"But MaryBob, you don't know what has happened to me in the past."

"You don't know what I've been through."

You're right. I don't, and it may have been horrific. But what if all that has happened to me was just to show me what I don't want to help me decide what it is I *do* want? If I'm going to use my imagination anyway, which we all do, why not use it to imagine a life I would love to live? Again, how many times have I said, "What if....," and then followed it with a whole pile of junk I really hope *doesn't* happen? Remember my saying previously to be careful *not* to use "What if..." to terrorize yourself? I somehow thought that my imagining the worst could shore up my defenses against it. Let's look at a few pitfalls we might have heard ourselves discussing in our heads. Then, let's flip those into a more expansive possibility. You game?

What if I lose my job?

Well, ok, but what if I keep my job, get really good at what I do, and make such an impression that the company decides to promote me?

What if I get sick?

What if I take steps to maintain my health, enjoy the benefits of those good feelings, and live to be a hundred? How will I feel with everyone clamoring around me wanting to know how I did it?

What if I lose all my money?

What if I can use my imagination to feel the flow of money coming in, going out, and coming in to my life? How does it feel to be in the position to help those who need what I can offer?

What if they don't like me?

Ok, well, what if they love me instead? What will I do when I receive more invitations than I can fit into my schedule?

What if _____? There it is again. I can fill in that blank with all kinds of self-defeating verbiage, or I can turn it on its head and come at the situation from an entirely new angle. The real question is, which one *feels* better? I kind of like the better-feeling thoughts myself. My mother used to say that some people "enjoy misery." That expression used to make me smile when she said it, until I became that person. The ache felt familiar, so I held onto it. My story rolled over and over in my head. I baked it there like it was a precious family recipe handed down through the generations. What I found myself cooking was a meal of discontent. Better yet, I ate that meal over and over, thinking it was nourishing me.

We all have options, and my own experience has shown me results going both ways. Personally, I got tired of myself. After three full years of crying every day for any number of "poor me" reasons, I had had enough. How my dear husband tolerated my butt is beyond me. He says now he knew the real me was in there somewhere waiting for the right moment. Talk about the patience of Job! That moment arrived, and I recognized that I needed to change my own thinking if I was to ever have a life of joy and love again. There was still mud on the path to that realization.

Dying for Healing

Six months after arriving in California my devoted sister called to let me know our mother was near death. With the choices I had made earlier, I had put myself in a financially-compromised position so I couldn't afford to buy a ticket home. There was no one to borrow the money from, so there I sat two thousand miles from home fearing I would never see my mother again. I know, I was the one who had made the choice to leave my home town, but I had not bargained on my mother dying before I had a chance to sit with her ever again. My lifelong best friend, and I couldn't find my way to her death bed.

You may or may not believe in the sudden apparition of angels, spirit guides, or the idea of divine intervention, but I experienced just that the very next day in the form of a never-before-met neighbor. Her wings weren't sticking out of her shirt, but they were in there somewhere. Being so far out in the foothills, and to make it easier on the mail carrier, our collective mailboxes were at the end of a long dirt road. She found me there crying. After explaining to her my need to get home in time to see my dying mother, she asked if I would like to use a buddy pass she had been given by a friend. I almost fell onto her shoulders in relief, so after much rushing around, a long drive to the airport, and a flight delay of over eight hours I arrived in Ohio in enough time to see my unconscious mother pass from this life to her next. I was disconsolate. Numb.

Even the death of our mother did not change the temperature inside the local freezer. One of my most precious memories of that event is of my former father-in-law. As I walked away from my mother's grave on my way to the car, he touched my arm and said, "MaryBob, why don't you stop by the house sometime and see us? We'd love to see you." He'll never know the power his kindness had for me in that moment. Leaving my mother next to my father in the cemetery, I could do nothing but stare at the floorboards of the family car. Silence. Two days later I returned to California. My friend Bill stood waiting for me at the gate and put his arms around me as I wept. Little did I know then, he and I would create an extraordinary partnership.

Bill and I had come from two different ends of the country and somehow found our way to each other. I was angry, hurt, and thrashing my way toward a new existence. Thank God, he had already learned of his connection to the Universe and of his ability to acknowledge and forgive his past. He radiated inner peace while I raged on. He recognized the flaming darts I hurled in his direction were not about him. They were my undeveloped skills of recognizing my own worth and true power. He had a dream of our creating a life together. He envisioned it being like nothing either of us had experienced to date. I couldn't see it yet, but went along anyway, hoping against hope that his pipe dream would come true.

Silver Lining

"There are always flowers for those who want to see them." – Henri Matisse

When You Need a Friend

Bill and I had met on the phone, while he was encouraging me to continue my studies with ELI. He talked to me like we were old friends at the fair. His southern accent threw me off a bit. It made me smile. We had come to a common point in our lives, but from two entirely different worlds. Neither of us was convinced we had anything more than a friendship, but we had a strong shared goal — to learn to see our worlds anew through study and practice. He consistently listened as I poured out everything, allowing it all to land safely, with no judgment.

I had spent my life trusting everyone and everything around me. I had been light-hearted, easy going, and confident. Suddenly, I could count on one hand those whom I trusted at all, and it felt as if I were crawling on my hands and knees, afraid to look up. I judged myself for every move I made, but blamed it all on everyone outside of me. The joie de vivre of my former me left me standing in the middle of the road. I internalized the opinions of others and felt sorry for myself all at the same time. Lovely combination.

Bill somehow saw through all of it, and after my best tirades against some triviality I had blamed him for would ask me in a calm voice, "Now, what are you really mad at?" The first time he did that, of course, it sent me to whole other level of anger, but after digging deeper I saw there actually *was* another truth underneath the one I was raging so loudly against. Let me give you a real-life example.

For years, I tried to mend the relationships back home. I called in on every holiday hoping for a breakthrough. It was Thanksgiving, and I had made the call, imagining my loved ones gathered around the dining room table, but the reception was the same. It was another ghost call. Eventually, I stopped knocking on that door and let it go. That day I hung up the phone. Nothing. A day or two later, Bill suggested something which I heard as an effort on his part to control me. He could "have an idea," and I'd go to town with it in my head. I was sure he was trying to run my life, and off I'd go like a racehorse out of a gate. "Don't tell me what to do! You're not the boss of me! Stay out of my business! Oh lord, it could go on for hours. So, there he sat listening to me rant like a crazy woman in heat. After my steam ran out, he let the air be still for a moment then asked, "Are you complete?" I said, "Yes." He then asked me again, "So, what are you really mad at?" Well, it took me a minute, and I finally recognized that I was still holding onto my failed phone call. I blubbered it all out and onto him, and he just listened. As soon as I was finished, his idea took on a new light. In short, he created a safe place for me to be who I was, and over time he became "home" for me. I learned to recognize my own patterns, and with that recognition came the ability to choose differently. Ever so slowly my anger and hurt ebbed and peace made its overture.

On our way from the airport after my return from my mother's funeral, Bill suggested it was time for us to leave

ELI. The business had evolved, and clearly, I was too far from my daughter. I was determined to be more available for her, and that meant moving east. That evening we pulled out a map of the U.S. and asked each other, "Where do you want to go?" I determined I had to be east of the Mississippi River, and Bill, originating from the Gulf Coast, wanted to be in the warmer weather of the South. Both of us wanted an airport nearby, so Atlanta it was! We packed the car, put my dog Nellie in the back seat, and set off for Atlanta, stopping first in Chicago to visit my dear friend Paul, and then in Ohio to attend my daughter's annual dance recital.

Silver lining? I can't begin to describe the relief and warmth I felt upon entering the state of Georgia. I remember thinking that it felt like home. It was springtime, and there is not a more beautiful place than this state in the spring. The mountains, trees, flowers and more than that, Billy's family were a salve to my broken soul. We stayed for a week or so with his aunt and uncle while we looked for an apartment to rent. They did not know me from Adam's house cat (I've picked up a few southern sayings here). They were kind and gracious, and I really didn't know what to say, or how to act. I felt grateful and fearful all at once, in a state of observation and caution more than anything, keeping everyone at arm's length, just in case. I had become somewhat withdrawn, not my playful self, choosing to listen more and speak less, while attempting to glue myself back together silently, and Billy's family took me in as their own. They may not know the appreciation I felt for all of them until they read this book, at which point I'll agree to discuss it. Why wait? I'm working on being less outwardly emotional these days.

We found a place to live and began a new life in the big city, one day, one breath at a time. What's remarkable is I made great new friends and created a new "family." How? Who knows? They were and still are the sunshine behind my once-upon-a-time cloud. The new surroundings and new friends gave me air to breathe. I studied new concepts, old concepts, and mostly myself. I can't count the hours, days, weeks and months spent in the North Georgia Mountains, hiking and sitting while working through some emotional or spiritual possibility of what life could be. Walking the paths through the trees I imagined how my life might look with peace as the focal point. I began to consider the possibility of a life consciously chosen. I reveled in our discussions of ideas and concepts instead of people and circumstances. Silently making my way to waterfalls and overlooks gave me the space and quiet to mold my thinking, which in turn birthed feelings of appreciation. I have read studies of the powerful effects that spending time in nature has on the human psyche, and I am here to tell you, there is nothing like it. I hugged more trees than I can count, thanking them for being there, a sedative to an anxious spirit. My friends and family gave me the moniker, "tree-hugger." It's literal, not figurative.

I examined old habits and beliefs and physically felt the constrictions of some of them. I realized parts of what I had learned were for me, and parts weren't. I began taking yoga classes to expand my mind, body, and psyche. My definitions of ancient words like, "God," and "heaven" were expanded and became inclusive. I realized the power of my own mind in determining the outcomes of my life. Living with a vision in mind replaced living in response to my circumstances. I learned to appreciate the writings of Siddhartha, the ideas contained in the Upanishads, the potentialities within Science of Mind. In all of it I fostered a growing appreciation for all forms of belief and with that a relaxation into the experience of being human.

Beautiful Mud Pies

Did you ever make mud pies when you were little? We made them by the dozens, and when the mud and stones got too thick we'd add water to loosen it all up before we sprinkled dandelions on top as decoration. My childhood home was surrounded by beautiful flowers, but picking them for mud pies was not a good idea, so a few dandelions had to do. I remember pouring in the water before mixing, and the stream would make a little hole in the middle. As I poured, the water spread across the top leaving the goopy mud below. The thicker the goop, the more water I added. Eventually, I stirred it all together and carefully added the flowers before presenting my creation to my always-appreciative mom or dad.

That's what I think I did when we came to Atlanta. I allowed my goop and stones to lay on the bottom long enough to go looking for life-giving water in the form of work and friends, and then stirred it in until it was just right. I had been working on a new spiritual and emotional approach to life. One that felt expansive and inviting, and yet letting go of my former constricting beliefs was, and still can be, a process. *Just keep adding water, MaryBob. Keep adding water.* Seek that silver lining because you know it's there, but only if you really want to find it.

I listened to a few others telling their stories of woe, felt the energy of those tales, heard myself in their words, so decided to become a teller of uplifting stories instead. I wanted to begin choosing where I put my mental and emotional energy. I knew there was some tiny morsel of good in whatever had happened in my life, and in that process, I discovered that the morsel of good wasn't so tiny after all. Some people wear their "poor me" sagas like a badge of honor, ever seeking to evoke pity from the person listening.

I get that. I do. I know there are horrible, tragic stories everywhere. I know people suffer, and I recognize the power of compassion. I also know I may choose to live in my sorrowful stories for a minute or for a lifetime. It's a choice I can make. I am clear now that my revisiting my contractive feelings only serves to perpetuate them in my own mind and body. Once again, this was not an overnight, *flip the switch* kind of move. It still takes some effort to move myself away from a really *juicy* story, but it gets easier every time I do. We humans are some kind of *wonderful*, aren't we?

I also believe we can find the good if we only look for it. It may not jump out at us, and the road to it may be relentlessly challenging. I still believe it's there. If it's not obvious, I make something up. I'm serious. If I ask myself why something happened, and nothing comes to mind, I make up a reason to get my brain working from a different angle. Let me give you a couple examples:

Remember my losing the "Mother of the Year" competition by leaving my daughter in Ohio? Well, she and I spoke on the phone frequently, and we saw each other every few months. I tried to get comfortable with our being separated, but could not. Three more years passed. Eventually, I stopped crying over it, and decided there must have been a reason for our separation. I chose to believe that we would each find strength despite the five hundred miles between us. One glorious day she called and asked if she could come live with us in Atlanta. Hallelujah! I had dreamed of that day, not wanting to make the decision for her and choosing to believe that any work I did on myself would pay off for both of my children. It did, it has, and there's still more.

My worldview was not what she had known it to be. I believe her arrival precipitated an acceleration in my healing, and over time she grew to love the South. Nothin' like chicken and biscuits for breakfast! Therein lies another fragment of the silver lining. If I hadn't made the move I did, slogged through the mire of my own mind, much like the crawl to freedom in "Shawshank Redemption," her experience of life would have been entirely different than it was. She found friends here who love her dearly, and developed a comfort in her new home. She is today delighted and happy here, thank God, so that is the part of the story I choose to focus on. When thoughts of those painful moments years ago cross my mind, I intentionally shop the shelves of my mind for thoughts that feel better. No point in reliving that which felt destructive.

Another practice I've learned came from Billy. Shortly after arriving in California I received a speeding ticket while driving his car one day. I was *sure* he was going to be upset at my carelessness. Not so. After I tearfully related the details (who cries over a speeding ticket?), he said, "Well, I'm grateful for that policeman. I think he may have saved you from hurting yourself or someone else. This is a blessing, not a problem." I couldn't believe my ears. Say what? Could you please repeat that again for me? I was speechless. That one incident was a screaming example to me of our option to choose our perspective in any situation. Sometimes it's easy. Sometimes it's not.

Was it all unicorns and rainbows here in the Bible Belt? Not exactly. Recall that I had just abandoned my conservative Catholic upbringing in favor of that mind-bending metaphysical/spirituality stuff. As much as I loved my new-found thinking, even I had to admit it sounded a little "woo-woo." The bookstore shelving devoted to such ideas was tiny in those days. It was the early 2000s. Over time that space grew as more seekers like me, found comfort there.

Shortly after divorcing and long before leaving my hometown, with the situation as it was, I developed a desire to "hear" from my long-deceased dad. I was sure his response to my choices would have been different. I had been reading about a spiritual medium, who was having success receiving messages from the dead, so I told my mom I was going to New York City to see her. At first my mom looked at me like I had three heads, asking me if I really believed that was possible. I explained that I did believe it, and after more explanation as to why I believed it, our conversation ended. Get this. I went home after having spoken with my mom, and my message light was blinking on my phone (remember it was 1998). It was a message from my mom saying that she was wanting to go with me to New York to see the medium too. Are you kidding me?! She had somehow worked her way past the admonitions in her own mind, and wanted to go with me. I was astounded and thrilled. That conversation felt like the days we used to enjoy together. In the end she couldn't go, but it would have been great to explore the many worlds of belief with her. It was rare for her to wander so far from what she had believed her whole life. She was a remarkable woman.

Wow, so here I was in *Georgia*, the perfect testing ground for my newfound status as spiritual explorer, don't you think? Thank God for big cities where anything and everything can have its place. I discovered that cultural differences are not experienced only in foreign countries. The language may have been the same, but the art of living in the South came from an angle unbeknownst to me. Get ready. Here we go!

The Baby with the Bathwater

"Sometimes you will never know the value of a moment until it becomes a memory." – Dr. Seuss

My Spiritual Allergy

Please don't mention or even indicate that you might consider mentioning words like "church" or "sin" or worse yet "priest! Please. Just don't. I may very likely develop an allergic reaction, the likes of which has never been witnessed. Does someone have an epi-pen handy?! For real. And spare me the "Lord and savior" stuff. My system can't take it. You're kidding, right? Boy, you have really drunk all the Kool-aid! I can't believe you did that, and I'm relatively certain you and I are not going to be friends. No way."

If you read all the way through that previous paragraph, just know that that was me twenty years ago. My rough patch had left some deep wounds, and I wasn't sure the scabs were ever going to fall off. The healing underneath was not quite complete, particularly when it came to organized religion. Those were some shoes I had already walked in, and no matter what my dad had said, I was done. Throw those damned things off and fling them into the deepest ocean no matter the cost! In fact, if possible, take aim, and throw them *at* someone who continued to believe all that dogma bullshit handed down by those wanting control more than they wanted to help people. That was my view. I was sick to death of any and all mandates originating from that book of fairy tales they called the Holy Bible. Do not quote scripture to me! Although Catholics are not prone to quoting the bible, I had had my fill of it all. I had yet to investigate the commonalities sewn into the fabric of many ancient texts, including those texts sourced by my newfound spiritual teachers. I also had not yet encountered the concept of a universal spirituality, which honors all religions and creeds. Interpretation is everything. I had just recently begun to study for my private Ph.D. in "Personal Belief Systems," and had completed only the intro and 101 classes. The prerequisites for advanced study came only through life experiences, one at a time.

The irony is I bumped up against a group of strong *believers*, and made a choice to work with them. I was looking for an occupation that would inspire me and push my skill set. I missed being a teacher. I had to find some type of work that gave me the chance to meet new people. Religiously I could not have been more in disagreement with the dogma to which this group adhered, but as human beings, they shed a new light for me on the term "Christian." They actually practiced what they preached. If reference to one's religious beliefs had made me uncomfortable in the past, I was about to grow some thick skin. Initially, I squirmed and ranted (inside my own head) every time I heard the word "Lord" or "Christian." For those of you who have not lived in Dixie, allow me to illustrate how common it is here to speak of your religious orientation.

After moving to Atlanta, I reconsidered my decision to not teach and took a position at a local high school. I thought I'd give it one more shot. I had worked for a hospital, a university, and from home. In desperation, I had become a barista at Starbucks and learned to create every combination of coffee, milk, and flavorings. My pride was hurt, and I began wondering if I had resigned 4 years earlier because of my life circumstances at the time, or was I really over the teaching gig? I discovered a pride I didn't know I carried when mentioning to someone that I had been a teacher for twenty years. I missed the kids. The local county school system was enormous compared to what I had been used to, so I felt a little like a country mouse in the big city. Oh, what the heck! Let's give this a shot. Remember, I came from the public schools in Ohio where Church and State ran different directions on the educational highway. Crossing the median strip could be fatal for teachers and students alike. In my twenty years in Ohio classrooms I could not recall one student making any kind of religious pronouncement in front of the room. Not so in The South, as I learned in my Spanish II class one day.

I had instructed my kids to give a brief presentation to the class using the future tense in an explanation of his/her upcoming plans. "I will…" was the scaffolding for their practicing the sounds needed to master this concept. The class was small, and all went along *normally* in my opinion, until one of them commenced by saying, "I will become a missionary, and I will bring the word of God to the world to save their souls through the knowing and accepting of Jesus Christ as their Lord and Savior." Her word selection was impeccable and her pronunciation stellar. I thought, in that moment, my own skills in Spanish must have been slipping. Did she just say what I think she said? This is a *public* school I'm in, correct? I sat pasted to my seat, frozen in time and space.

In my mind's eye, I can still see my blanched face and feel the blood rush to my feet. I believe I decided to remain in a paralytic state so as not to noticeably jerk any of my body parts. How was I ever going to prepare myself to address the class with a cover-up explanation sufficient to rescue that poor child from the onslaught of abuse that was "fixin' to" get heaped on her? Well, no need to worry about that in the land of cotton. Said 'onslaught' never materialized. She finished, sat down, and the class casually turned their heads toward me to see who was up next. I was gobsmacked. Truly. Not one kid rolled their eyes, and I never heard a single snicker. I'm relatively certain I did a poor job of covering my catatonic state, but nobody said a word. Yep! I was for sure in the Bible Belt now, and at that time my recognition of it rubbed my nerves raw. I was still in the throes of believing that to be "anti" anything might prove beneficial, particularly if it was "anti-organized religion." It took everything I had not to roll my own eyes and snicker in derision at that precious girl. Clearly, I had more work to do. On myself.

Spiritual Renewal

I had been more than willing to allow the bath water containing my religious upbringing to circle the drain and fall fast. Yes, it touched every aspect of my life. What was once clear had become murky over time. I recalled learning to scuba dive in the muddy water of a local quarry, eyes and mouth protected by a mask. When I later dropped into the Gulf of Mexico, the clarity allowed for a whole new world. I was in some murky water, and I obviously needed clarity. I had to be careful here. In the few moments following my student's presentation I had an argument within myself. The angry, flailing me wanted to walk directly to the front office and submit my resignation. I then recalled the "babies" in the bath water of my former training. The love, compassion, and desire to help, which were such strong components of my upbringing.

Was I willing to sacrifice those beauties while flushing away the *no-longer-true-for-me* facets of my earlier years? Was I so hell-bent on being right that I would let all of it float away, then wish I could pull it all back in later? It was not an instant revelation, but eventually, I decided to ransack my way through the heap of old teachings and pluck out those that I thought might serve me well in the future. I didn't have to agree with or even like what was left in the pile. I only had to pull out what may have been valuable for a new look see. What did I pull out? Compassion and understanding for starters. At the time, I had a seriously low supply of both, so when I chose to look at them, I saw they needed to be dusted off, then polished for a new shine. This was going to be a concentrated effort to see the world differently.

You could not have convinced that closed-off me that there was even one redeeming quality about anything remotely *organized religion-ish*. Not one thing, and like a good family member who claims to hate her siblings, I also became highly defensive of my own religious heritage, if anyone else tried to join me in my disdain. Now, how convoluted is that? I can rip my old catechism to shreds, but you just need to take a step back, if you think I'm going to stand here and let you criticize it too. Fasten your seatbelts, Everyone. We are in for an exciting ride!

Once again, why do we do that? Why, when we decide for or against something or someone, do we feel the need to turn and bash what we just evolved from? Why can't we simply look at all of it, discern which delicacies we'd like to taste, put those on our plate next to the leftovers we saved from before and move on? I mean, our plates are all different sizes, platters even. Can't we believe what we believe today, add to or take away from it all as we go along, and know that we're never going to get to the end of the buffet line?

No doubt, my life experiences affect my views of the world and for the most part lead me to a broader understanding and acceptance of another individual's circumstances. I remember using my father's illness as a reference when one of my students was struggling with her own parent. I recognized in that conversation my own ability to push against adversity as an opposing force or to remember the value of it to be used to help someone else later.

I also recall standing in my kitchen as one of my dear friends gingerly broached the subject of her being lesbian. She was fearful of my response, terrified that I would not allow her to be with my children. It was the early 90s, and I had not yet had the opportunity of knowing someone with a different sexual preference. My heart wrapped itself around her, and once again, my mind was broadened. Later I would thank her for bringing to me a worldview I hadn't known. Future students and friends would be the benefactors of her trust in me at that moment.

Isn't that what life is about? I've heard of "the wisdom that comes with age." That's what I'm talking about here, right? It was easy to be all puffed up in my own youthful self-righteousness with my one bowl of chocolate ice cream, perfectly frozen and sprinkled with my favorite topping. I could eat that forever, if my body would survive, but I probably wouldn't grow to be old and wise. My body needs variety for strength and flexibility. Is that not also true for my mind and spirit? Don't I do better when I'm open to possibilities I never before considered? Doesn't having all the answers in advance spoil the joy of the discovery? The question is, how do I respond to the entire buffet of life itself? Have I evolved enough to stand back, knowing that the road I'm on is eventually going to branch off into something new? Do I stand in my one spot, damning all the others who see the world differently? Do I smack those views to the floor because I don't understand, and I don't want to understand? Or do I take a good look at all the offerings and choose, calmly, those items I feel drawn to? In my mind the evolution lies in choosing calmly, knowing we are each here for our own growth, however that may look.

I don't believe we are ever going to know it all while in these human bodies. Done. Finished. I got this. That is, of course, unless we do. Still at the buffet of life, I may know someone whose plate is so full, they can't consider even one more option. They've decided theirs is the only way. Now, I get to decide if I can spend time with them, without wanting to change them. Can I hold onto my own joy and not go down the hole of judgement?

I see personal uncertainty in the individual who demands to be heard, who shouts her beliefs or who harshly argues. Yes, of course we all have differing personalities, some quieter than others. I'm not talking about personalities. I'm talking about the need to proclaim personal beliefs at every turn. If I continually find fault in others, I believe I am as uncertain of myself as he or she who vehemently claims to possess the truth about God, Universe, or Spirit. We would all like to be certain about what we believe, but can we be? I'm not sure. My husband frequently says, "We may not get what we want, but we always get what we expect." Expectation *is* belief, right?

My beliefs are a result of thinking something over and over again. Experiences play out in my life according to my expectations, so that's it. I can only be certain for myself and my impressions are a result of my own experiences. I am in no place to tell you what specifics to believe. I can only share options that may or may not resonate within you. It is always up to me to choose and then choose again.

I was determined to never — and I mean never — do some of the things I did in the past, like set foot in a church again. My mother always told me, "Never say *never.*" I now agree with her. I was also unwilling to engage in a conversation about the good qualities of some of those people who had *wronged* me. I was so furious about my own experiences I couldn't see straight. Still, I wondered how I would ever feel choosing to pass by a well-known cathedral and not opening the doors just to make some ridiculous philosophical point to myself. And what about all the precious moments that had filled my life?

Recently, while on vacation, Billy and I passed by a small historic Catholic church in Michigan just as Mass was starting. It had been 18 years since I had last stepped into a Catholic church, and I was curious to see if there was still some fizz in that bottle over what I had been taught. Would I feel the need to carry on about how wrong they were? We decided to go in and have a seat. I was testing myself. I want to tell you I felt like a grownup as I observed my response to what was being read from the pulpit. Did I agree with the lector? No, I did not, but I looked around at those in attendance and recognized that we are all one. We come here for our own experiences, and although I was not in agreement with the lesson, I was in love with the idea of the rituals and the shared intent to feel the presence of the Divine. I even lit a candle in honor of my mother. She was smiling, I'm sure. I knew in that moment I would not have to wonder any longer how I would ever relate some of my most precious memories to others without feeling that cutting sadness. I had graduated from my own school, and now the search for deep joy could begin in earnest. Finally, I concluded that any reservation on my part was my own issue. I couldn't invalidate the previous decades of my life. I had to find the joy that was surely present during that time. I felt proud that I had indeed found some of the peace I had been seeking.

Seeking Your Peace

I can still feel the sting of anger when old stuff comes up. It doesn't happen as often now, and the sting is not as sharp. Maybe someone mentions something that used to irritate me or maybe an old friend reminds me of an escapade I had hoped he'd forgotten. Maybe my husband uses a phrase I disliked as a child. The opportunities are endless. The ten-year-old in me can pop out at any time, particularly if I feel someone is trying to control me or if I hear a harsh tone of voice. One of my favorite trigger points is being asked why I did or didn't do something. That one question used to send me to the moon and back. I heard it as a challenge to my choices, and that did not sit well with me. I can't even tell you who it reminded me of. All I knew was that you'd better have a damned good reason for asking. I eventually recognized my immediate snappy reactions, and said to myself, "Self, this is not a good sign. Your battery still has some charge, so you'd better get to work on *you!*"

Maybe pushing so hard against an old memory or an unpleasant experience is my higher-self telling me to take some goodies and leave others behind. That anger is only a cover for fear. What is it about all that old stuff that scares me now? That was then. I'm grown now. No need to be afraid of being coerced. I pick. I decide. I'll bet there was some good in all of that, and by tossing it *all* out I felt vacant in places. I did. Not vacant like "I needed to go to church" vacant, so all you church-goers can just curb your enthusiasm. Vacant like it didn't feel good to be so *against* what some people believe, to be judging some believers for being so judgmental. Read that last sentence one more time. I felt vacant because I was judging people because they were being judgmental. That's messed up, right?

Those are some knots that needed to be untied right there! In seeking my own peace, I had to allow others theirs, even if it came in the form of religious dogma or preachers shouting from the pulpit. I could see that my sharp scalpel was no longer needed. I began to see the beauty in what remained. When I put down my boxing gloves, I found I was more inclined to hold hands with my old self and with those who had chosen to stay the course or strongly believe in a divergent path. We really *could* be friends after all.

During my personal coup d'etat, I remained relatively non-verbal when it came to expressing my views on life. Generally, I practiced formulating my emotional and spiritual views with my husband only. If I started to express an idea and got stuck in my own sentence, he would help me find the words to fill in the blanks. He and I talked ad infinitum and still do about varying approaches to spirituality and emotional awareness. A close friend of ours says he and I have existential discussions on a regular basis.

Much as a child learns a language, I was reworking my way toward self-expression. Only rarely did I share an alternative possibility with a coworker or friend, knowing that my view might not mesh with hers. I still carried a fear of rejection. That was a bag of rocks I would haul around for a long time until I recognized myself doing it. I was particularly cautious at work. I was happy to be there and not about to make waves. I remained true to myself, but quietly.

Here's how I saw it; My earlier experiences with people claiming to be Christian or at least in some way affiliated with any church had been more than disappointing. In my mind, despite their "faith," those people were ruthless, unforgiving and vengeful. I hadn't gotten to know this new work crowd yet, and for all I knew this could just be another version of the same thing. As a protective measure, I was going undercover. I believed in the *heart* they put into the work they did, and I enjoyed their company, minus the Jesus, Lord and Savior stuff. They didn't ask me what I believed, and I didn't say. I was lying low. They were openly expressive of their religious views, which was something new for me. Oh, yes, there were moments when I considered running for the hills, but I somehow knew that staying was where my growth was. Their shoes were much like those of my father's when it came to treating all people with dignity, and I felt an inexplicable comfort and familiarity with them.

Heavenly Father

Speaking of how my dad treated people, let me tell you a story. My dad grew up one of ten children and as a young boy was sent to live on a farm with his Uncle Henry and Aunt Laura. I was never sure why. He said they sent him there to fatten him up because he was so skinny. We eventually came to believe that his parents simply didn't have the wherewithal to raise ten children. In any case, he loved that family, and I think they were the ones who laid the framework for his love of all people no matter their station in life. Earlier I told you about the St. Vincent de Paul store he started for the less fortunate.

As my father's health declined, my mother finally had to admit she couldn't handle his needs any longer. His mental and physical decline used up every ounce of energy she had. She reluctantly found a convalescent home for him, not knowing he would be there only one week before he released his body. When my dad transitioned at age seventy-four, he was fittingly laid out in his own funeral home. The place was packed with visitors, and we family members were all standing in the room as people came and went, offering us condolences. We wanted to be sure we acknowledged everyone, so we kept our eyes on the front door and my dad's casket.

At one point, we noticed an unfamiliar man standing at the casket, tears pouring down his cheeks. He had obviously not showered in days, wore tattered clothes and held a brown paper bag with what appeared to be a bottle of liquor inside. He just stood there staring at my dad's body for the longest time weeping. We all looked at each other, not knowing what to do, so eventually, I walked over to him. "Hi, I'm Bob's daughter. Did you know my dad?" "Nope. Not really. Just wanted to pay my respects. He's the only man to ever pick me up off the street and buy me a hot meal. He didn't even know me. Just wanted to come and say thank you and goodbye." As you can imagine, mine were the tears that flowed then. Examples of my father's deep love of humankind don't come any greater than that one.

So, let's get back to my job. Ok, I'm surrounded by "say-it-out-loud" Christians feeling like a private investigator with no real assignment. They somehow knew not to ask me to say any blessings before big meals, and when invited to their weekly bible study I gently declined. Words like "fellowship" and "devil" gonged against the inside of my head causing me to breathe deeply and silently to quiet myself. I knew my energy was screaming, but I thought they couldn't hear. In those moments, I reminded myself that we are all one. Days, weeks, months and years passed, and I became attached to the owners, my coworkers and their dedication, work ethic, and humor. I remained cautious and quiet in conversations revolving around religion.

Another coworker and I had become great friends, and a group of us, maybe fifteen or twenty, attended the funeral of her beloved father — in a church of course. I was not crazy about the idea of going, but this wasn't about me. I remembered the comfort I felt in the support of friends at my own father's funeral, so no matter what, I was going. During the entire service, I was eavesdropping on a conversation between two little "birdies," one on each of my shoulders.

"I don't think I can sit here and listen to this. It's infuriating."
"Oh, get off your high horse and just listen! It won't hurt you, and it may help if you'll just try and hear what the message is without getting all worked up about the context."
"But..."
"Hush!"

The service was over, and naturally, Kathy had gone to the cemetery with her family. One of my coworkers didn't feel well, so we waited in the empty church for her husband to come and pick her up. As we waited we chatted with each other, and out of the blue one woman raised her voice to say, "Hey, Y'all, I have an idea. How 'bout in a few weeks we all go together to get MaryBob baptized and then go to brunch at that new restaurant near my house?"

STOP! What?! All eyes were on me, and I may have forgotten to breathe in that moment. The silence was deafening. There was no escape hatch through which to fall, so there I stood, statuesque, I'm sure. Man, these Southerners are relentless, aren't they? If passing out had been an option, I would have taken it! A few seconds passed, and she then laughed, so I did too, nervously, followed by the others. Well, shit! I guess that cat was out of the bag. I must not have been as inconspicuous as I thought, and yet I felt love from all of them. I was ok with them and apparently, they with me. It was one of those moments when the world leaned a little crooked on its axis, and to be honest, it was a relief. How could this be? I simply loved these people. The assorted flowers in my garden had taken root, and the blending of colors felt surreal.

TO HAVE LOVED AND LOST

"What we have once enjoyed deeply we can never lose. All that we love deeply becomes a part of us."
– Helen Keller

The Lessons of Love

You know I could go on and on about the number of people, the relationships, the events that were no longer swirling around me, but what was most interesting was what I lost in all my searching, and that was my belief in myself. I had lost the 'me' who felt she could do anything she put her mind to. The 'me' who had unbounded curiosity about all things different and new. The 'me' who felt she had something to offer this world. I lost her. After the deaths of my dear friend in high school, my parents, my only sister, my first love, the virtual deaths of my family, friends and foundational beliefs after the divorce, I was not sure who I was or where I belonged. Was there even a place to live out my days that didn't sting with the blisters being chafed?

Feeling victimized by everyone and everything around me was one thing, figuring out how to like, much less love, myself was another. How could I ever forgive myself for the emotional pain my choices had caused any number of people? I think that is where I really got stuck. I had been such a good lifelong student in the classroom of guilt. I was much like the elephant tethered to the small stake in the ground, capable of a greater contribution to the world, but held in place by what I had learned to feel about myself. I couldn't see my good. I could see only my dark side, and the more time I spent focused on it, the worse it became. I had yet to realize that the power we have lies in where we place our attention. I simply couldn't shake the feeling that my having given into my own pain had been a great weakness on my part. I should have known better. I should have done better. I should have been better. I should have … over and over.

That word "should" is a troublemaker in any language. If you enjoy rehashing your past choices and feeling the pain of them, I suggest you use the word "should" on a regular daily basis. It will do the trick! With this one word, I successfully adhered my present to my past so any chance of forward movement was virtually wiped out. I anchored myself to regret, and sucked out any potential joy that might have been lurking, waiting for a place to express itself. Seriously, I cannot think of one single (I know that's redundant) usage of that word that does not ring of judgement.

Oh, I know there will be readers who might argue that "should" keeps us in line and out of scrapes. As in, "I should go home now before I get into any trouble." Ok, there might be an argument for that usage, but what I'm referring to is the "should" we use against ourselves and others. It's a self-inflicted judgment for not being good enough or an assumption that we are privy to the life path of someone else. Is it possible that what I should/should not have done was what I needed to propel me to another level of understanding? Is it possible that the choices others made about and around me were the catalysts for my growth?

Are you stuck to a "should" and haven't taken a step forward yet? Have you super-glued yourself to the past, worn the badge of honor for having suffered some personal injustice, and are now trying to figure out why the hell your joy meter is stuck on "low battery" instead of "fully charged?" Think about it. You and everyone else may be doing your very best. Maybe the new skill you're asking for is one of self-acceptance. Trust me. It is a skill, and it takes practice. I was so comfortable with the pain of self-incrimination. It was the "devil I knew." Self-acceptance is a little patch of fresh grass. It is much sweeter and life-giving than the street drain I had been circling.

Billy and I learned the judgment behind that one little word, and we decided to remove it from our vocabulary. Not using "should" makes for an interesting sentence structure, particularly when I really do feel like judging someone. Kidding. Well, maybe a little. One of our favorite adages is, "Everyone is doing the best they can, in any given moment, with the skills they have. If they could have done better, they would have." That includes me. So, we threw the "shoulds" out the window. That idea felt a lot easier when applied to someone else. Not so easy to let myself off the hook.

When I reflect on my past, I know that it was never my intention to cause harm. Not ever, and yet I did. I know that. When I imagine walking in their shoes, I can see it. My forgiveness work has been as much about forgiving myself as it has been about forgiving others. It took me a long time to believe that my own beliefs are a choice, not something I was forced to hold onto. That includes the thought that I deserve to be punished. Through the years, I had seen too many good people, including young and old, who believed poorly of themselves. One particular acquaintance of mine was "happily married" until the day her husband left her. That was over twenty years ago, and she is still holding onto the resentment and regret for what "should" have been.

She blames her former husband and ultimately herself for every failure since then. Today she is in her sixties, makes a meager living, has little social life, and wonders why she is so alone. It seems to me that she has attached herself to the "I'm not good enough" life script, and spends her days and nights "shoulding" all over the place about her past and present. Any potential joy finds it hard to squeeze in there among the weeds in her garden. She says she wants to be happy. A lot of us say that. The question is, am I willing to do something about it? There is no room at the table for "happy" to take a seat in her home. With her insisting that she is not good enough she is closing the door on her most cherished guest, and squashing the gifts she could bring to the party.

For many years, I was stuck in the past too, so began my deliberate choice to see not only the good in others, but the good in me. If I ever wanted to be the greatest expression of myself in this lifetime, I simply *had* to focus on my own good, understanding that the kinder I was to me, the kinder I would naturally be to everyone around me. On the rare occasion when I read or watch the news I marvel at how unforgiving we are as a society. We are hypnotized with the feeling of righteousness. One news story and the *shoulds* start flying like sparks. We think we know what is best for someone else, and we believe that knowing holds power for us. I wonder.

Feet on The Ground

If you come from a small city in the Midwest and have entertained ideas unlike those of your upbringing, you may have felt the pull of deeply guarded ancestral values. I'm not saying it doesn't exist in the other parts of the country. It's just uniquely powerful in the conservative, hardworking agricultural belt. That same area that grows the kindest, warmest, easy-going version of mankind. I know it's my story, and maybe I'm being myopic, but the small-town, close-to-the-earth, tight-knit communities of the Midwest had, for me, a generational flow and expectation that held me lovingly. The traditions and rituals of a shared ancestry were the glue that held us all together. Even if a stranger entered our midst, we would find a way to incorporate them into our community as part of the natural flow of our open-heartedness.

Just the other day I had yet one more acquaintance remark on how people from the Midwest are his favorites. He said we're forthright, honest and keep our feet on the ground. I was basking in his compliments until that last little thing about keeping our feet on the ground. I heard that as, "They stick with what they know to be true, and don't make waves." You're allowed to think I've taken it a bit too far with that, but at least read the next paragraph before you jump to conclusions.

We "keep our feet on the ground." Ok, how do you hear that? What exactly does that mean to you? To me that means that old ideas are the best ideas. Playing it safe is more important than taking a chance. Better safe than sorry. Challenging what we've been led to believe is heresy. I mean, thank God the Wright Brothers, John Glenn and Neil Armstrong didn't "keep their feet on the ground." Literally. And I'll bet Thomas Edison wasn't his teacher's favorite student. His mother, a trained teacher, pulled him from public school to home school him because he couldn't behave himself. These Ohioans went against the grain, and in the end contributed immeasurably to our culture.

Keeping my feet on the ground meant staying put and staying quiet. It meant being the example of "play your cards right to arrive safely at death." That's a paraphrase of one of my favorite Mary Morrissey statements. Don't you love that? It meant living my entire life just like I saw others living theirs. Quietly, according to the books, so inside the box that packing tape was not necessary. I believe I mentioned one of my friends saying to me when it all fell apart, "People are angry with you because you're doing what they want to do, but they don't have the guts." I wanted to hug her across her desk. My point here is that no matter how strong the gravitational pull, nor how harsh the consequences, I knew in my heart there was another way to see this experience we call "life," and I simply could not be stopped from searching for it. No tradition, heritage, need to please or fear could bind this spiritual quest. It just was what it was.

What I have *not* lost is the love that surrounded me for all those years. It's not lost because I carry it in my heart and mind. Because of it I am a card-carrying member of the "I Have Been Well-Loved" Club. I choose not to allow the tattered ending of that life chapter negate the entire story. There was too much delight throughout. It took me a while to see it like that. I used to feel only the loss of it all and not the gratitude for the memories. I could only lament "what could have been" instead of acknowledging having had the joy and learning of the experiences in the first place. I know the strength of my foundation was my launching pad, and I also know there's a landing strip somewhere with my name on it. Where? Time will tell.

Another something I would hear my loving dad say was, "The Lord helps those that help themselves." I know that can sound judgmental, but he used it more as an incentive for me, when I was wanting something from him and was unwilling to do my part. If "Go ask your mom" didn't work, dad would fall back on the former. It must have stuck in my head because helping myself get out of my own funk was exactly what I decided to do. I was way too young to spend the rest of my years coasting down the path to death. The veneer I had worn early on had been shaken loose, so I made the decision to remove it all together.

Part of that removal was the decision to remarry. Billy had asked me if I was interested, and for years I had said simply, "No. Been there. Done that. Got the T-shirt." Eventually, we made an appointment with a minister friend of ours, who pointed out our common intentions. She spoke of the power of two people united in a common dream, using the "Wherever two or more are gathered" verse from the Bible. It was the first time I had heard a Biblical verse without having my habitual allergic reaction. It made sense. Several months later we married in a small private ceremony. Our vows were homemade, committing to effort on our part one day at a time. They had no resemblance to the vows each of us had spoken on multiple previous occasions. Through my fear, I felt a calm in all of it. I felt "at home." That home might still have had some rooms that needed to be rearranged, but the overarching sentiment was "peace." Finally. I sometimes see in my mind's eye our relationship as that of Tevye and Golde from *Fiddler on the Roof.* If you Google the song "Do You Love Me" from that play, you'll hear how their connection grew over time. Our start was one of practicality, necessity and intention. I may not have "given him children or milked his cows," but I have "lived with him and fought with him" and can't imagine my life without him. I tell him he's "my favorite somebody" in those moments when I'm not trying to control him. Still working on that *desire-to-control* part of me. Billy is such a good sport when I lapse into the old idea that I can control anyone, particularly him. He, for some reason, gets a kick out of me when I'm all fired up about something he has or hasn't done according to my specifications. Once again, it's not about him. It's about me and some thought I have running in my head, usually it's an approval issue. I have worked diligently to let go of that need, and there are still little confetti pieces of it stuck to my brain.

Billy was the only one who knew how intensely I was struggling, searching under every rock for a piece of my own puzzle. Over time I came to recognize and acknowledge my deep desire to come from love in every interaction. Always. I can hear Tiny Tim singing *Tiptoe Through the Tulips*, and it makes me smile. I'm not saying I'm an Olympian yet, but the desire is there. My connection to the Divine is there. My job is to stay aware of that connection and to operate, moment to moment, from that place. To come from love, knowing that this human experience is going to give me opportunities to practice forgiveness every day. Forgiveness of others and myself. Small stories of forgiveness help me build a strong foundation.

I'm going to oversimplify here, so bear with me. I have had a question for myself over the years that flashes like a neon sign. I've made a food analogy of it, of course. Food always works. So, here is my question; On my last day in this body, am I going to be happier that I got to taste rich chocolate truffles with cream filling even if the milk was occasionally sour, or am going to wish I had only ever had Rice Krispies treats my whole life? I mean, I like those treats, but a whole lifetime of them feels boring at best. Oh tedium! I'm relatively certain I'll go with having tried the rich truffles with the occasional sour milk, and I feel the same way about having had great adventures along with having lost much of my family and friends all those years ago. Get it? Only now, looking through the lens of my previous experiences can I recognize a dark chocolate truffle when it shows up! If my life had been pleasantly vanilla in its entirety, it would, in my opinion, have had little depth or breadth. Who knows? It may all turn around one day. My family, friends, and I may one day find ourselves sitting around a table marveling at our individual life journeys. As always, anything is possible. In the meantime, I recognize that any disappointment I feel or have felt is a choice on my part. I can only be disappointed if I choose to be, and the same is true in reverse. Choosing disappointment surrenders my power to another. It pinches off my connection to my own divinity. It is not life-giving.

Now don't misconstrue my intended meaning. I am not advocating going out and stirring up trouble just to shake things up. I am saying that we have the option of seeing our sorrows much like we see getting into shape, only for the soul. Our bodies give us a signal, and with effort and possibly some pain, the results are life-changing. We learn to crave that which is good for us, even brussel sprouts, instead of getting hooked on the sugar high we get with a steady diet of anger and condemnation. We rarely distinguish how good we do feel until after we don't. It's in the "don't" that we recognize the "do."

Some of us make a habit out of looking for trouble in our lives. We get a rush out of finding what's wrong with someone else or some situation. The more times I tell a story, the more the feeling of that tale becomes a bad habit, and habits can be undone. I'm convinced that my nervous system got used to the vibration of "drama" and sought it out like addicts seek their drug of choice. This drug may be legal, but it's just as debilitating to our lives and spirits. We can get so very used to the "high" of drama that we feel we can't exist without it. Our part in these crises becomes a statement of our value. My favorite example of this is a group of mothers sitting around discussing who had the most traumatic experience of child birth. What? Is this really a contest? How is it that we feel a satisfying jolt from being the one to have experienced the most pain? I don't get it. Or maybe I do. Maybe we tell those stories to help us feel stronger, more durable.

Lessons to Live By

Everyone loses someone or something eventually, in a dozen different ways. We know this, and no matter our philosophy on life, the experience is painful. Best friends and old loves can transition unexpectedly along with parents and siblings. Divorce, another kind of death, has its own brand of grief, and simple but firm rejection by friends and family still another. What's the point? In my weaker moments, I'm not sure there is one, yet when I'm feeling I could take on the world, I see the richness provided by those loves and agonies, and what I learned from them. What did I learn exactly? I like to remind myself of the following;

1. I learned that nothing stays the same no matter how much I want it to, and in the end that is a good thing. With the change I'm forced to grow, not just grow up, but grow out. Out of my smaller previously-held worldview and into a broader perspective. How would I ever have discovered those people and ideas I now hold close to my heart, if it weren't for the loss I experienced first?

2. I learned that my way is not the only way. Yes, I'll remain true to me, and in the meantime, I will enjoy the many, many shades of color it takes to form the beauty of this world. Most importantly, when my view

does not necessarily blend with that of another, I'll sit back with an art-lover's eye and contemplate the possibilities.

3. I learned that every moment counts. I could say "don't waste any opportunity," but that reeks of fear, so I prefer to frame it as "savor the moment." I used to be fearful of saying I was happy or of being vulnerable expressing "I love you" to someone who didn't expect it. Not so much anymore. The vision of Snoopy with his joyful nose in the air spinning pirouettes comes to mind. That's a little extreme, although I do like the thought.

4. I learned that everyone has a story to tell. Each individual has the option of using their experience to heal and inspire or to draw in continued sadness and pity. Should I choose inspiration as my ultimate goal, I believe I will know deep emotion and satisfaction. There is no tale worth telling that is without a profound rolling of the tide. No movie or novel worth reading is without the highs and lows to keep us entrenched. It's part of living on this planet.

5. I learned that life is not happening *to* me. It is shaped *by* me. By my thinking. There's a lot more to this belief, and suffice it to say I have come to know that my thoughts about every little thing matter. I can be lazy and let all kinds of scary thoughts run rampant in my head, or I can think on purpose. I am always at choice. Yes, this takes effort. "I don't have a choice" is a sentence that fell away from my vernacular years ago, because I do always have one. I may not be in love with the entirety of my options, but the choice is still available to me. This one little ditty has spun me on my head more than once. It takes away the

pleasure of my victimhood. Do things still happen that I don't really much appreciate? Yes, occasionally, and therein lies my opportunity to try on another pair of shoes, either someone else's or a style that might give me another take on my own life. I really would like to again feel comfortable in a pair of stilettos! Not kidding.

Back to the story:

The days, months, years passed as I examined myself, my beliefs, and my emotional responses to life. I read and studied, laughed and played, worked and dreamed my way to a comfort zone of sorts. I remember one sunny day walking through the front gate of our apartment community and recognizing that I felt happy and confident. It was a feeling I hadn't had in years. It swept over me like a spring breeze. I smiled, and in recognizing it I felt a profound sense of gratitude. The expression, "I'm back" came to mind. I knew that the *me* that was back was not the same me who had taken that wide left turn years earlier. This latest version had had some of her dents and scratches buffed out along with a new paint job. She was not the latest model, but there was a certain surety to the road she had chosen. It was as if the cells of my body suddenly remembered a delicious feeling. I wanted to grab hold of it and not let go. It was fleeting, but it was real.

Wasn't Built in A Day

"Great things take time; that is why seeds persevere through rocks and dirt to bloom."
– Matshona Dhliwayo

Reassembling My Life Brick by Brick

I have a dear friend my same age who told me once about an experience he had. It seems to fit here in my story. He was one of fourteen children born to a couple with little means of survival. The family lived on a twenty-acre piece of land owned by his grandmother. An uncle who had helped take care of his grandmother in her later years convinced his mother to leave him the land, and her only request was that, upon her death, he would give one acre to his sister with a family of sixteen. The uncle did as he was asked, only the acre he bestowed on them was located at the other end of the property, and they had no means of moving their current house or building a new house. The father had recently suffered a stroke and had few options, so he instructed his seven able-bodied boys to dismantle their two-bedroom home. They then hauled the bricks and wood in wheel barrows across the field to the other end and put them all back together again in the form of their *new* house.

This new house had a basement, one bedroom, and a kitchen. The ten boys slept in the basement on two beds, and the four girls slept in one bed in the kitchen next to the table and wood burning stove. The work was grueling. The days were hot. I have no doubt those seven boys had second thoughts about that little project. I could imagine there were other things they would like to have been doing. In the end, the sense of satisfaction they felt at completing that task stayed with Ronald forever. He said he loved, over the years, to hear his father brag on him and his brothers, about how they had rebuilt the family home. Can you imagine doing such a thing? The resulting new house looked different than the original. It was now home, and they were grateful.

That is a great metaphor for my last twenty years. My philosophical, spiritual, and familial houses had been dismantled brick by brick, and reconstruction was challenging at best. I looked over the pile of rubble that was once my life and wondered what to salvage and what to throw away. What would I take with me on my journey? At times I wasn't sure I had the energy or the chutzpah to build a new life. Part of me felt like lying down on the gravel and curling up, but in my heart, I kept hearing my husband saying, "It's going to be ok," so I got back up. Initially the *easy* days were few and far between.

During those years of reconstruction, my employment pattern was all over the place, until I finally landed on solid ground with my "believer" friends. What a ride! In the meantime, I was doing all I could to get my proverbial "shit" together. I dove into encouraging my daughter in her new surroundings, meditating, walking, journaling, listening, and sought joy around every corner. Solidifying my own framework was my goal. What really were my beliefs, and was I going to be responsible for my own emotions or was I again going to depend on the opinions and influences of others to determine my value?

I listened to audiobooks and voraciously read philosophical, spiritual and metaphysical books by a plethora of authors. Among my favorites were Deepak Chopra, Neal Donald Walsh, Bruce Lipton, Marianne Williamson, James Redfield, Esther Hicks, Byron Katie and Mary Morrissey. These and many others filled my mind and heart. I couldn't get enough!

Day in and day out. I watched the movie *The Secret* over and over, attempting to absorb and apply all that it inferred regarding how our thoughts create our reality. I attended conferences with Dr. Brian Weiss and John Maxwell, leaned into Oprah's "Super Soul Sunday," practiced yoga, and spent more than a little time in nature. I was determined to find my own truth about this existence of ours, knowing full well that my truth may not jive with what I had learned in my early years.

In retrospect, I can see how hard I worked. I was swimming upriver in rapids hoping to hook a log with one of my arms. As strange as it sounds there was a certain exhilaration in discovering new ways of seeing the world. Over the years, I came to know that my pain was temporary. I made myself climb up and over every hill because I knew there was a new something to be found on the other side. At least most of the time, right? The power of speaking now from what took years to decipher and discern is indescribable. The delight in knowing there will always be more is delectable. I would recommend this search to everyone. I also have come to believe that it doesn't have to be so grueling. In my case, I just didn't know any other way. I'm hoping the words in this book will encourage you to seek your truth so that you too find comfort in your own discoveries.

Letting Go of the Sugar Coating

We would like to build our relationships and careers and belief systems in a day without all the drama that comes along with running over nails and screws, but I believe a portion of those experiences is a prerequisite. How can we know *up*, if we don't know *down*? Or *hot* if we don't know *cold*? We can't. Sometimes we walk straight into a fire and other times we stand outside and just watch someone else's. The ebb and flow are a necessary part of growth, and both take time. I remember being so desperate for clarity that I sat down one day at the office in California and announced to the owner of the company that I was ready to take any measures necessary to be *finished* with my emotional upheavals. She smiled at me and said, "MaryBob, it doesn't work like that. Life will bring you all sorts of opportunities for growth, one at a time. At some point you'll have the chance to take advantage of those opportunities or not. It will be up to you. We can't do it all here and now." I was so bummed.

Along the way my children asked me questions I had few answers to, and although I could easily flare at a long-held unwanted belief, I struggled to verbalize what I *did* now believe in. It was as if I held all of my newfound world inside and some unknown speech impediment lay over my desire to express. I had not yet let go of the fear of reprisal and rejection. For years I kept most people at arm's length. If I didn't let them in, they couldn't hurt me. They couldn't shut me out.

I wasn't conscious of my doing that until my new favorite friend Kathy called me out on it. We were walking the neighborhood one evening, and somewhere in the conversation my fear jumped up. She looked at me and said, "MaryBobby, are you scared of being rejected again, 'cuz it sure feels like that to me. Why don't you tell people what you really believe instead of sugar coating it in case they disagree?" I think I stopped in my tracks. She was right. I was still operating out of a sense of fear instead of a sense of trust. I've heard that awareness is the key to choosing a different behavior. In that moment, I became aware. She instructed me to just shine my light. I heard her then, and I have shared that idea with others. What a gift she was then and is to me now.

Did I do that? Yes. I held some deep beliefs that might scrape the raw edges of someone near me, so when they espoused *their* beliefs, I fell in line like a good little duckling. That was fear, plain and simple. It was not a bad thing. It was just a thing, and staring into its eyes caused multiple physiological reactions: Hiccups, the need to pee, sweaty palms and feet, twitching eyelid. Any number of unexpected bodily repercussions, all potential escape routes.

Over time friends and coworkers began to ask my "take" on a variety of situations. I was startled at first, so "caution" was the name of the game. I didn't want anyone to get all flapped up about anything I said. I wanted to help when asked and speak in words that could be heard. More than anything, I wanted my friends and children to see the world as a field of pure potentiality as Deepak Chopra describes. The best analogy I can think of for that field is the internet. We all know the internet has infinite potential to hold information, and when we search an item, it comes to our computer because we "call" it onto our screen. We can "call" information that feels good and not so good. We can call information that lifts our spirits or throws us into fear. I believe the same is true for our lives, only the search box has been laced with years of our conditioning, so we think it's *normal* to expect the other shoe to drop. Calling up what we would *love* takes lots of practice, on a daily basis.

Our conditioning is a result of our culture, our families, our religious upbringing, our education, our choices in the past, any number of influences that we have allowed to carry weight with us. So, if I am seeking a particular "something," and my search box has been laced with the expectation that that "something" is impossible to attain, then my results will prove my expectations to be correct. On the other hand, if I can recognize the influences in my search box, reframe and reorganize their impact, and choose to remain focused, expectant, and emotionally charged, my chances improve exponentially. Literally, anything is possible with enough belief, attention, emotion, expectation, and action, I believe.

I know. Some of you will be feeling your blood pressure go up at that last statement, thinking I've lost my mind. I don't think so. Don't we all know of instances where individuals created something out of nothing? Recovered from a "fatal" illness? Won races without having legs? Painted masterpieces with their toes? Those individuals believed in their own field of pure potentiality. If that term doesn't sit well with you, call it something different. The bottom line is we are all creators, and we will create either accidentally or on purpose with what we allow to occupy our thoughts and thus our emotions.

With that idea in mind, the confines of my previously held beliefs, based on fear of retribution, were slowly dissolving, and the confidence I needed to express myself began to take form. The many questions from my newfound *family* gave me practice time, and gradually, the words began to flow. In fact, I now can get so enthusiastic that I force myself to apply the brakes. I don't want to bowl them over. I remind myself to deliver new ideas in bite-sized pieces, lest the listener choke and spit it all back out. Remember, Rome wasn't built in a day.

Lost in the Woods

I can't say that every one of us has passed through a similar tunnel, but I have a sense many of us might have rubbed elbows with someone who is hidebound, not willing to consider another way of thinking. If you're reading these words, and if you answer "yes" to any of the following questions, I think there's a strong possibility you and I have both felt lost in the woods at one time or another. I'm telling you now, you don't have to stay in the fog forever.

1. Can you remember a time when someone asked your opinion, and what came out of your mouth wasn't "the truth, the full truth, and nothing but the truth?" You coated your answer with satin, afraid that the wool of your truth might scratch?

2. Have you ever felt like rearing up at someone else's truth being pushed on you, only to look around and see everyone around you nodding their heads in agreement with the speaker? Damn! Talk about feeling "special!"

3. Do you just *know* there is more to this thing we call "life" than what you've experienced so far, but "just be grateful for what you have" keeps coming out of the mouths of those loved ones with whom you're sharing? Squashed like an acorn on the sidewalk!

4. Do you find yourself lowering your voice with words like "energy" and "manifesting?" Worried that your crowd will think you're falling off your horse? Oh no! Here comes the New Age stuff!

5. Does your taste in movies and TV shows run counter to that of those around you? The violence you used to be able to stomach is just too much now. You wanna watch what?!

I've heard that timing is everything, and I believe that to be true in many cases, not all. The question is, "Whose timing?" If I feel compelled to do something, do I wait for the timing to be right for those around me, or do I go with my own timing? *That* is the sixty-four-thousand-dollar question, and you *do* have the answer inside of you. *Lost in the woods* is not a forever thing.

Back to the story…

For me, each revelation led to the next. At times I was thrilled with the possibilities and at others angry with myself for any number of reasons. Through it all the learning was equally explosive and minute, joy and drudgery, philosophical and practical.

My delivery from diffidence to confidence resulted in a sort of notoriety for me as resident philosopher-comedienne. In taking the time to excavate my own difficulties I learned to see and feel the motives of others. I found I could walk in their shoes, if only for a few moments, and that little walkabout allowed me the grace to choose my responses to them. Note the word "choose" here. I had chosen to shut myself up long enough and simply be in the room with others, not saying a word. In doing that I learned to listen more and speak less. Don't get too worried here. I still love to talk, hopefully now with a bit more deference. In the listening I remembered to breathe, and therein lies one of the keys to effective communication. Breathe. Everything is delivered a little more effectively with a breath or two beforehand.

To Thine Own Self be True

"The individual has always had to struggle to keep
from being overwhelmed by the tribe. If you try it,
you will be lonely often, and sometimes frightened.
But no price is too high to pay for the privilege of
owning yourself." – Friedrich Nietzsche

Remember Your Self Whole

How many selves do we have? Well, for me there was the daughter self, the wife self, the daughter-in-law self, the mother self, the teacher self, the friend self, and the whatever-was-leftover-after-all-of-that self. It's true, right? We all have the roles we play in our lives, and those roles either enrich our lives or drain the life right out of us. Some of the selves we chose either consciously or unconsciously, and others are chosen for us. Many of them serve us well most of the time. Occasionally the roles take us over, and we get "a hitch in our giddy-up." Another expression I learned here in the South.

What does a hitch in our giddy-up look like? We keep getting sick for no apparent reason. We dread going to work. We find we're impatient and can't explain why. We find fault with everyone and everything. We argue at the slightest provocation. We stop exercising. We're tired all the time. We're bored. There are hundreds of red flags, but most of the time we forge ahead without stopping to ask ourselves what's up? We go to the doctor, start drinking energy drinks, Google our symptoms, blame our circumstances.

I'm urging you to just stop. Stop and look around you. And I mean really look, a couple of times every day. I say look around you, but what I really mean is look inside of you. Are you the Energizer bunny on autopilot, moving so swiftly you couldn't smell a rose if you were knee deep in them? Are you at all conscious of the small "goods" in life? The dog sleeping contentedly next to you. The teenager at the drive through window who gives you an extra biscuit at no charge. The stranger who makes eye contact with you and smiles? Try it. Try staying alert today to the little stuff. When you go to bed tonight, look back and feel those little moments. Choose five moments from the day and bask in them. This practice has now become a habit for me, and I find myself smiling when I pull the covers to my chin because I know the next few minutes will be a happy time inside my head and heart. Try not to say, "cheesy" when you read that last sentence. Falling asleep with a smile on my face beats the hell out of figuring out how I'm going to tell someone off the next time I see them.

And about that "look inside of you" idea. I am so serious! Are you trying to be all things to all people? Is there something you're doing that just doesn't work anymore? Is there something you'd like to do that you haven't? Ask yourself the tough questions. I'm not talking about a 30-second commercial break from your regularly scheduled programs. I'm talking about a series of intentional, on-purpose, time-alone meetings with yourself. In your current life, what's working? What would you change if you could? What are your deepest core values? Are they being met? Is what you're doing adhering to those values, or have you fallen off the track?

I know I can do anything I put my mind to. It took me a long time to acknowledge I could *not* do *everything* in one lifetime. That came as a bit of a shock and with some disappointment. Oh, and let me add *relief* to that list. I really did want to do it *all*. In this lifetime. I wanted to have the warm home and family life, be the business woman, the dancer, the adventurous jungle-trekking explorer. I wanted to save the children of the world, learn to speak at least five new languages through cultural immersion, and let's not forget become an author-speaker-teacher. And I was hoping to make them all full-time experiences. I worried that I would run out of life before I got it all accomplished. I'm relieved to know now I can have some of these lives on a full-time basis, and the others as side shows. After a lot of introspection, I came to realize what really mattered to me, and the peace in that discovery is beyond gratifying.

The good part about wanting to do it all was my insatiable curiosity, openness to new ideas and willingness to take risks. The bad part was I failed to sit long enough and take the time in my earlier years to really look inside of me to see what I believed. Oh, I'm sure I did a little self-check here and there, but questioning my authority figures was not an option. Life was generally peaceful, so why put a stick in the spokes? With few exceptions, I did what was expected of me. I think smoking weed was about as far off course as I ever got in the early days, and it was a blast. Shhhhhhh.

Societal, familial, and religious influences are powerful forces. Our culture determines what is right or wrong, good or bad. How can we begin to see the world through another's eyes if we stay under the same influences we've known our whole lives? Don't we owe it to ourselves to dig and dig until we literally feel the presence of truth? The joy of discovery? The relief of peace?

For me cultural and religious diversity was as far as I would go, and only as a bystander absorbing the ways of those from a different ken. I attempted to teach my children and my students acceptance and kindness. I attempted to impart to them the desire to explore the world with its countless traditions, dialects, and beliefs. I'm sure I was successful with some and not so much with others. Back then I was all about everyone else's distinctions from me, their unique approach to everything life had to offer. I had yet to own the distinctions between me and myself, the places in my life where I was living others' expectations of me and not my own personally determined values.

I believe now that it all happened perfectly. It wasn't always pretty, but it was magical. If I or any other person had chosen differently, chances are good that I would not be sitting here writing this sentence. I could very well have forfeited the opportunity to find the beauty imbedded in all the belief systems previously unknown to me, to learn to see the world differently, and to find my ever-changing place in this universe. Not only did I find ideas different than my own, I found in myself an understanding of those ideas I spent years railing against. The terminology may be distinct, yet the underlying intention is the same.

With one person responding differently than they did I most likely would have missed the beautiful relationships I have today, with my husband, my children, my coworkers, my friends. One of those gems is my love for my husband's ex-wife. Billy threw the two of us together in that retreat almost twenty years ago thinking we may have something in common. Little did any of us suspect that Julie and I would become lifelong friends. She and her family have become part of ours. We call each other "wife-in-law" for lack of a better term when introducing ourselves to strangers. The connection is simply remarkable, and the three of us are pretty darned proud of ourselves. I could have so easily missed out on the opportunity to have them all in my life.

Looking back now I see that my dive into the mud wasn't about my marriage or the response of my family and friends. It wasn't about the Catholic Church or the town I grew up in. It was about *me*. I simply had to figure out who I was outside of the confines of those institutions and circles. The term mid-life crisis has come up more than once, along with the eye-rolling that accompanies the phrase, "finding oneself." I don't believe it was a crisis, although I did at the time. For me it was a reckoning. Where had I been, and where was I going? Could I gladly anticipate my next decades of life standing inside the framework I had built around me? For me the answer was, "No." Walking this path has been worth every step, and I trust there is more.

Peaceful People/Peaceful World

I have this belief that goes something like; If every person in the world knew themselves to be the powerful spiritual individuals they are, then we would have a more peaceful world. I know. I know. Sounds pretty damned lofty and more than a little naive, but think about it. If you and I really understood ourselves and were grounded in our own beliefs, then what you said could not offend me or hurt me. You could not disappoint me, nor I you. If more of us trusted in our inherent divine nature, the need to overpower or hurt another would not exist. I'm envisioning and feeling the joy of that kind of universal belief, that tipping point through mass consciousness. Imagine that feeling with me. Sit with it. Know your powerful connection to something more than what you see with your eyes or hear with your ears. On a basic level, we all know that individuals who harm others do so because they are unhappy with themselves. They do not see or feel their own value and connection to a greater purpose. If I love, respect, and value me, I am not going to lash out at you.

I feel that the force that some call "evil" is proportional to the *disconnect* one feels from their God, Source, Universal Spirit. Call it what you will. The weaker the connection, the more intense the "evil." Making the effort to know our deepest heartfelt desires and taking steps toward them is one road to a deeper spiritual connection and thus world peace. Lofty? Maybe. Impossible? I don't think so. Anything is possible. I have told my children to remember my saying that long after I've traded in this body for a newer model. Try that idea on for size and see how it feels. I'm betting you're going to like it. The world *is* a field of infinite potentiality.

If you ask my children, they will tell you that I became a better mother after tough self-examination. The questioning brought answers, and the answers brought peace. Yes, there were rivers full of tears. Oceans maybe. And I probably walked the circumference of the earth more than once while mentally and emotionally processing some situation or another. I learned to take responsibility for my own emotions. It used to be easy to blame someone else for my feelings. Now I know better. The only one responsible for my happiness is *me*. At those times when I felt struggle my sweet husband would encourage me to go take a walk in the woods to find peace. Taking walks has never failed me. Something to consider.

They say that music has powerful effects on the psyche. The genres are ever-changing and ever-evolving along with the dance moves to accompany them. So it is with each of us. You may have danced swing way back when, and now you'd break dance, if your body could make that happen. Do what you do, and do it with all your heart. Don't half-ass anything just because someone may be looking and may not like it. Know that you are an ever-evolving being, so what you believe today may be different than what you will believe twenty years from now. That's the beauty of evolution. It's okay. What's the point in living our days in these bodies, if we are just going to do the same thing over and over? Particularly if we avoid something because we think we're going to be judged by someone or something.

Gurus and Diets

It occurs to me that some readers may see themselves at different points in the emotional passages I've described here, and others may feel no connection to this story at all. Isn't it the same with gurus and diets? As much as marketers, friends, or family would like us to believe that some *one* thing is good for everyone, we know that is not possible. If we are all here as individual expressions of Whatever You Want to Call It, then there is not one guru who has all the answers for us. One may instruct me to meditate with my feet on the ground and another with my legs crossed, sitting with eyes closed or walking a labyrinth. Nor is there one diet that works for everyone. All protein, no carbs. No fat, no animal products. Cooked, raw. If I make the decision to know what works for me up front, I may not feel the need to counter or to be offended by someone else's view. It seems we love being offended by the words or actions of others. To me, it's exhausting. I would rather sit in my own truth and let them have theirs.

So, I've determined that it's my job to hunt and peck the points that work for me and maybe offer them as an *option* to those who indicate interest. My suggestion? Every idea is just that, an idea. I get to choose my response to that idea and adopt it or not. When I feel myself getting flapped up about something, I know the answer is inside of *me*, not out there. That may sound philosophical, and sometimes it's just plain annoying. There *are* times when I'd rather *not* take responsibility for my emotions, even when doing just that might prove beneficial for everyone concerned.

Take the time to examine what you really want, what you really believe. Be a seeker. Find others who are seeking too, whether they agree with you or not. Don't be afraid to make a mistake. Identify exactly what you are afraid of, and turn it around. Ask yourself, "What would I love?" Please don't stuff your curiosity to not make waves. The more you stuff, the bigger the waves in the end, until you have tidal waves. Tidal waves are deadly. The sooner you do this self-inquiry the better. That way you will be less likely to find yourself later all tangled up in the brambles of what others want for you and at a loss for how to extricate yourself painlessly.

All of what we've learned we've learned from someone else. Thank heavens for the many teachers who have taken the time to offer us their talents and ideas. Run like lightning with those ideas that make you smile in anticipation. Keep after the notion that you can do anything you put your heart and mind to. Looking forward, back and all around, recognize and acknowledge the good you see, particularly inside yourself. Do what you must to keep your focus there. Is it easy? Not always, but it's doable, and the more you do it the more you'll do it. It does get easier. Draw you. Dance you. Solve you. Work with purpose on those things you love. Who cares if nobody around you loves it too? And learn to learn from you. Take the time to sit quietly every day. Just sit there and breathe. Every aspect of you will thank you. Talk to your younger self. Tell her/him it will all be okay. Talk to your older self. Ask them what the next move is. Allow that older self to talk to you.

Every relationship we have is a bridge. Some personal, work, friend relationships may be momentary or they may last a lifetime, and I believe each one takes me to the next. The same is true of my relationship with myself. What is that ever-present force that breathes me and keeps me moving? For me it's not my personality or my body. Some call it God, Universe, Source. For me it has become the all-accepting, never-judging love, the unseen forces that are ever creating through me.

Most of all, have the imagination of a child. Take the time to daydream your life into reality. You're a creative being, and every building, song, car, piece of art, dish, sock, and mansion you see either around you or on some screen was created in someone's mind before you ever saw it with your eyes. What would you love to create in your mind? Start down the road toward it, and see what happens. Stay awake to you. Listen when you hear yourself say, "Yes!" Listen to those who encourage you. When I tell you that the world is waiting for you, I'm not kidding. With the achievement of self-knowledge, the joy of self-appreciation, and the belief in the power of Life itself, anything is possible. Please, give this world your greatest expression of you! Allow me to repeat myself. Anything is possible, and you are the one to make it happen.

FURTHER READINGS

These are some of the books I read at the time. The authors mentioned have since published many more books also worthy of your attention.

Pema Chodron: *When Things Fall Apart*
Eknath Easwaran: *Conquest of Mind*
Neal Donald Walsch: *Conversations with God* (Book 1) and *The Little Soul and the Sun* (Children's book for adults)
Deepak Chopra: *The Seven Spiritual Laws of Success*
Brian Weiss: *Many Lives Many Masters*
Rosemary Altea: *The Eagle and the Rose*
Bruce Lipton: *The Biology of Belief*
Eckhart Tolle: *The Power of Now*
Caroline Myss: *Anatomy of the Spirit*
Rhonda Byrne: *The Secret*
Gregg Braden: *The Isaiah Effect*
Louise Hay: *You Can Heal Your Life* and *Heal Your Body*
Byron Katie: *Loving What Is*
Daniel Goleman: *Emotional Intelligence*
Raymond Charles Barker: *The Power of Decision*
Ernest Holmes: *The Science of Mind*
Dr. Michael Ryce: *Why is This Happening to Me… AGAIN?*
James Redfield: *The Celestine Prophecy*

Bio

MaryBob is a wife, mother, and grandmother who began her journey with a BA in Education and Spanish along with studies in Mexico, Spain and Costa Rica. Her travels and studies resulted in her becoming a collector of stories. Life itself has been her muse.

MaryBob spent twenty-one years as a high-school Spanish teacher. She is a self-proclaimed people-lover, seeker, hiker, adventurer, tree-hugger, survivor, inquirer, researcher, meditator, humorist, story-teller, linguist, cultural appreciator, dancer, dog-lover, yoga practitioner, relationship consultant, irreverent wordsmith, idea enthusiast, cheerleader, hugger, suffragette, lyric-lover, and colorist.

She lives in Atlanta, Georgia with her husband Billy and their dog Blue.

For more information visit: www.marybobstraub.com

60918054R00112

Made in the USA
Columbia, SC
20 June 2019